Islamic Reassertion in Pakistan

Contemporary Issues in the Middle East

Islamic Reassertion in Pakistan

The Application of Islamic Laws in a Modern State

Anita M. Weiss, *Editor*

Foreword by John L. Esposito

SYRACUSE UNIVERSITY PRESS 1986

Syracuse, New York 13244-5160

First Edition

The paper used in this publication meets the minimum requirements of American National Standard for Information Sciences—Permanence of Paper for Printed Library Materials, ANSI Z39.48-1984. ∞™

Library of Congress Cataloging-in-Publication Data

Islamic reassertion in Pakistan.

(Contemporary issues in the Middle East)
Includes bibliographies and index.
1. Islamic law—Pakistan. 2. Islam and state—Pakistan. 3. Pakistan—Politics and government—1971– . I. Weiss, Anita M. II. Series.
LAW 305.6′971′05491 86-14337
ISBN 0-8156-2375-5 (alk. paper)

Manufactured in the United States of America

For Ali Razam

Contents

Foreword

John L. Esposito

For more than a decade now, much of the Muslim world has experienced the impact of an Islamic resurgence. Islamic revivalism has included both a greater emphasis on personal piety and the reassertion of Islam in Muslim politics. Both governments and opposition movements have appealed to Islam to enhance their legitimacy and attract popular support. Although Iran's Islamic revolution of 1978–79 is usually seen by many in the non-Muslim world as the beginning and paradigm for Islamic revivalism, in fact Pakistan provides an older and more fully developed case study of the concerns and issues which accompany the attempt to implement Islam in the modern state. This is due both to the origins of Pakistan and to its political realities during the 1970s.

The creation of Pakistan in 1947 as an independent nation and homeland for the Indian subcontinent's Muslims did not settle the issue of Muslim identity and independence; instead it proved to be the beginning of a decades-long quest and debate over just what Pakistan's Islamic character should be. For modern Muslim elites, Pakistan was simply a Muslim homeland, a state for those who shared a common historic identity and culture. However, for many other Pakistanis, including those religious leaders who had originally rejected the. Muslim nationalism of Muhammad Ali Jinnah and the Muslim League as antithetical to the transnational character of Islam, a state of Muslims must somehow mean an Islamic state. Although the new nation was called the Islamic Republic of Pakistan, its Islamic character was not systematically defined. Instead, an uneasy compromise was adopted. Pakistan remained a nation state indebted to its British colonial legacy for its institutions and the orientation of its elites. Its Islamic character rested tenuously upon ad hoc Islamic trappings—its title as an "Islamic republic" and constitutional provisions declaring that Islam was the state religion and that there could be no law contrary to Islam. In addition, the government supported religion through a ministry of religious affairs and retained a general sensitivity to religious issues. However, this approach was motivated more by a desire to control rather than promote religion.

Since the early 1970s the situation has changed dramatically with Islamic ideology, actors, and organizations becoming prominent features in political development as both ruler and opposition have often pledged themselves to the implementation of Nizam-i-Islam and an Islamic system of government. As a result, Islam has been used to legitimate changes in political, legal, educational, and social institutions. Elections have been postponed and political parties banned; Islamic laws, taxes, and banking have been introduced. To the extent that Islamic revivalism has meant an increased demand for more Islamically oriented states and societies, Pakistan provides an excellent example of the problems and issues which accompany the process of Islamization. Despite distinctive differences among Muslim countries, basic issues such as "Whose Islam?" and "What Islam?" exist for all. Who is to determine a nation's Islamic path—the head of state, bureaucrats, the 'ulema, intellectuals? What Islam, what interpretation of Islam is to be implemented? Will the interpretations of Islamic law developed centuries ago and preserved in medieval legal manuals simply be reapplied, or is there a need for reinterpretation *(ijtihad)* and reform? The tendency simply to reintroduce past answers, without undertaking a process of reform, has already raised serious questions about the status and role of non-Muslim minorities and women in more Islamically oriented societies. More generally, a review of recent events in countries such as Libya, the Sudan, Iran, and Pakistan reveals a host of issues. What is the nature of a modern Islamic government? Is the head of state to be selected or elected? How would the Islamic character of the state affect the qualifications for public office? What role will traditional notions of consultation *(shura)* and community consensus *(ijma)* play? What is the nature of Islamic law? Is it simply the interpretations *(fiqh)* of the past, or is a reformulation of law necessary? Or is it sufficient merely to guarantee that no law be contrary to the Qur'an or to Islamic principles?

Islamic Reassertion in Pakistan: The Application of Islamic Laws in a Modern State attempts to assess the actual impact of Islam upon Pakistani society. This is the first volume which analyzes and evaluates General Zia ul-Haq's Islamization program and its effect upon political, economic, and social development. The authors attempt to go beyond ideological rhetoric to determine what Islamization has really meant for political and religious leaders, for those living in the countryside, for economic planning, taxation, and legal reform, and for the status and role of Muslim women. The appeal to Islam in Muslim politics to strengthen national unity and identity, to legitimate policies and political actions, and to mobilize popular support will continue to be accompanied both by experimentation and by exploitation. Studies of Islamization programs such as that of Pakistan are important not only in themselves but also for their lessons for other such endeavors. *Islamic Reassertion in Pakistan* is an important addition to the growing literature on contemporary Muslim politics.

Preface

Today strong momentum exists in many quarters of the Muslim world to reassert Islamic principles in social, economic, and political spheres. This momentum often involves a quest for a new Islamic identity in the modern world, and may also include a redefinition of traditional Islamic institutions. Countries as varied as Pakistan, Tunisia, Saudi Arabia, Indonesia, the Sudan, Bangladesh, and Iran are all grappling with the exigencies of industrial expansion and economic growth in the context of the international economy. Along with this, these states are facing increasing demands for political participation by their respective populations. In many cases, they are responding to the cultural effects of development by the incorporation of Islamic principles and laws into their political and legal infrastructures. Yet there is limited consensus in the Muslim world as to what constitutes *Shari'a* (Islamic law) and what its role can and should be in a modern nation-state. Despite its current relevance, there has been surprisingly little research on the effects of the application of Islamic law, regardless of interpretation, on a contemporary society. Such is the purpose of this book.

This collection of essays by scholars from a cross section of academic disciplines and political perspectives is an attempt to understand the varied dimensions of the effects of one such instance of Islamic reassertion, as it occurred in Pakistan since 1979 (the year in which the current Islamization program was officially instituted). We have concentrated on institutional changes brought about by the Islamization program and their implications for Pakistani society, as these changes tend to have the most profound, fundamental, and long-lasting social effects. While proponents of change always have their supporters and critics, we have tried to overcome such biases by presenting differing viewpoints and interpretations of controversial issues in our elaboration of Pakistani society.

The first chapter provides the historical framework in which Pakistan's present situation is grounded. After overviews of both the basis of classical Islamic law and of the historical debate among South Asian Muslims on its social application, we address the form which this debate has taken in Pakistan since Independence in 1947. Although never officially supported in the past as it is today, the institutionalization of Islam into the political infrastructure has long been a subject of important discourse and occasionally of action. How Islamization in Pakistan occurred is viewed developmentally, showing that it was not simply a scheme dreamed up overnight by a military government to appease a hostile populace. Rather, the transformation was gradual, culminating in the official proclamation on 10 February 1979, that all laws—economic, political, and social—be put into conformity with Islamic precepts. We then review the significant legal effects of this decision, leaving analytical and ideological interpretation to the following chapters.

Hamza Alavi, in the next chapter, provides a historical interpretation of the effects of ethnicity and ideology on the formation of the movement for the foundation of Pakistan. He argues that it was not a religious movement per se, but was made up of diverse Muslim ethnic groups which rallied together in pursuit of decidedly material goals. He traces the importance of the "salariat" (an urban, educated class dependent on the colonial state) to the Pakistan movement, and elaborates on the various groups and ideologies which came to compose this movement. In his analysis of the influence of these Islamic ideological groups on contemporary Pakistan, Alavi contends that the true heirs of the Pakistan movement are the secularists who "reject and repudiate the idea of exploitation of Islamic ideology in pursuit of political ends." Islamic modernism is seen as no longer being a live intellectual movement, but rather as having been accomodated within secular political attitudes by the majority of the people.

The next three chapters analyze the effects of the legal shift to Islamization on economic issues. Shahid Javed Burki elaborates on what is meant by an "Islamic context" of economic management, which is a "fairly radical departure from the way the economy was [previously] being managed" in Pakistan, and identifies salient features of the economy being addressed by such discourse. In particular, he analyzes the extent to which the most recent Five-year Plan (1983–88) in fact conforms to the ideals and policies of the current Islamization program. Ann Mayer discusses how the program affects tax collection and subsequent economic implications. Analyzing the opposite end of the system—the distribution of new forms of Islamic taxes (i.e., *zakat*)—Grace Clark critiques the effectiveness of zakat and *'ushr* as a modern social welfare system in Pakistan.

Two groups warrant particular emphasis when discussing the sociocultural effects of the Islamization program in Pakistan: women and villagers. Women's options have been curtailed in their access to courts, education, and economic productivity, yet their response to the situation has been remarkable. Perhaps without the stimulation supplied by such circumstances, the Women's Action Forum and similar women's "consciousness-raising" groups would not have been formed nor seen as viable organizations. The "women's issue" has forced Pakistanis to rethink what Islam means to each of them, individually, and to decide whether or not they accept as valid the government's interpretation of it. This dilemma is most poignantly seen in the effects of the new program on the position of women. However, in the light of what Islamization could imply for Pakistan, it is interesting that Richard Kurin has not observed significant reinterpretations of tradition among the peasants he studied in rural Punjab. Rather, newly affluent villagers are contributing to the mosque very much as they have in the past. There are no reforms in village life, except for the crackdown on narcotics consumption. There do not seem to be any widespread changes occurring within the social fabric because of Islamization; the potential effects of out-migration by male workers to towns, cities and the oil-rich Persian Gulf may be more influential in the transformation of village social life.

Islamization programs and political motivations are interwoven throughout the Muslim world. In many areas, the reaffirmation of Islamic laws and values into the state infrastructure is seen as a way of defining national identity in the postcolonial world. For example, in his paper, "Explaining Revolutionary Islam" (presented at the Annual Meeting of the American Anthropological Association in Denver, 1984, page 23), Henry Munson writes that contemporary Muslim states do this because "viewing the world from an Islamic perspective inverts the subordination of the Muslim to the infidel in the secular domains of international politics, technology and economic development." Therefore, why the Pakistan government has chosen to identify itself with Islam and the political implications of this identification are of great importance, especially given the strong, centralized political structure of Muslim states today. In the concluding chapter of this book, William Richter analyzes the political causes and effects of the Pakistani Islamization program. He reviews the diversity of opinion on this issue offered here and elsewhere, and presents additional considerations for analysis.

As in all collective endeavors, many people have contributed to this one at various stages. The impetus for this volume was a panel I organized for the 1984 Association for Asian Studies Annual Meeting in Washington, D.C. Following that panel, many of us felt there was a need to systematically address the varied dimensions of Pakistani society which have been affected by the current Islamization program. Panel members Shahid Javed Burki, Richard Kurin, Bill Richter, and myself formed the nucleus for this volume.

I would like to thank the Center for South and Southeast Asia Studies at the University of California, Berkeley, for both moral and administrative support throughout. In particular, I am indebted to Bruce Pray, Barbara Metcalf, John Esposito, Bill Richter, and Bruce Lawrence for their intellectual stimulation and feedback on earlier drafts. I am especially grateful to Robert Bellah and Mark Juergensmeyer, who have helped me in innumerable ways to form my own ideas on the role of religion as a social force in the contemporary world. I would also like to thank my many Pakistani friends and colleagues, particularly Akbar S. Ahmed and Sabeeha Syed, who have helped me to understand various dimensions of Pakistani society which might otherwise have gone unnoticed. Susan Slyomovics, David Magier, John Foran, Claude Fischer, Larry Michelak, Andrea Press, Muriel Akamatsu and, most importantly, Ali Razam Khan, have all helped me in their own special ways.

I would like to thank the University of Hong Kong, and particularly David Levin and Thomas Wong of the Sociology Department, for their support in the final throes of getting this manuscript completed. Afsheen Ahmed provided invaluable editorial assistance, which is greatly appreciated.

Hong Kong A.M.W.
December, 1985

Contributors

HAMZA ALAVI is Reader in Sociology at the University of Manchester and Honorary Associate Fellow of the Institute of Development Studies at the University of Sussex. He is the author of numerous books and articles analyzing South Asian political transformations. He recently edited, along with Teodor Shanin, *An Introduction to the Sociology of "Developing" Societies* for Monthly Review Press.

SHAHID JAVED BURKI is the Director of International Planning at the World Bank in Washington, D.C. He was a Rhodes Scholar at Oxford University and a Mason Fellow at Harvard University. A member of Harvard's Development Advisory Service in 1973–74, he has also held posts as the director of the Rural Works Programme and Economic Consultant to the Ministry of Commerce, Pakistan. His publications include *Agricultural Growth and Local Government in Punjab, Pakistan*, and *Pakistan under Bhutto, 1971–77*.

GRACE CLARK is an administrator in the state of Maryland's welfare system. She received her M.S.W. and Ph.D. from the University of Maryland School of Social Work and Community Planning. Her dissertation analyzes the zakat program as a modern welfare system in Pakistan. Her research interests include social policies, systems to implement those policies, and the relationship between religion and social change.

RICHARD KURIN is the Deputy Director of the Office of Folklife Programs at the Smithsonian Institution in Washington, D.C. He received his Ph.D.

in Anthropology from the University of Chicago, and has taught at the University of Karachi as a Fulbright-Hays Fellow. He has carried out intensive field research in both urban and rural Pakistan, and has published extensively on kinship, religion, social structure, change and development.

ANN ELIZABETH MAYER is Associate Professor of Legal Studies at the Wharton School of the University of Pennsylvania. She has a Ph.D. in modern Middle Eastern History from the University of Michigan, a J.D. from the University of Pennsylvania, and a Certificate in Islamic and comparative law from the School of Oriental and African Studies of the University of London. She has studied Islamization in Libya, Pakistan, and the Sudan. Her work on Pakistan is based on research conducted in Pakistan in the spring and summer of 1982 on the impact of Islamic law on banking and taxation. She is the author of numerous publications on Islamization and the role of Islamic law in contemporary Middle Eastern legal systems.

WILLIAM L. RICHTER is Professor and Head of the department of Political Science at Kansas State University, where he has taught since 1966. He received his Ph.D. from the University of Chicago in 1968 and has written extensively on politics in Pakistan and in India and, more recently, on international security issues in South Asia. His current research is on geopolitical perceptions and international conflict in the region.

ANITA M. WEISS is Lecturer in Sociology and a Fellow of the Centre for Asian Studies at the University of Hong Kong. She received her Ph.D. in Sociology in 1983 from the University of California at Berkeley, where she taught various courses on comparative development and sociology of religion between 1981–85. Her dissertation and recent publications concern the interaction of culture, industrial development, and social change in Pakistan. She is presently researching women's conditions in the informal sectors of the labor force in various South Asian cities.

Islamic Reassertion in Pakistan

1

The Historical Debate on Islam and the State in South Asia

Anita M. Weiss

Dispute concerning the role religion should play in civil and political life has characterized recent South Asian history. In Pakistan, we find that dissension over the official role of Islam in the state is no new phenomenon. The sources of such disagreement lie in differing interpretations of classical Islamic legal theory and in the specific historical roles in which South Asian Muslims have found themselves.

This chapter begins by outlining the foundations of political authority in Islamic history as a means of introducing basic concepts and terminology which will be used later in the book. Issues have been selected on the basis of their relevance to the debate on Islam in South Asia. Following this section, the chapter provides historical background and introduces themes which have followed the debate on the relationship between Islam, Islamic law, and the state in pre-independence South Asia and later in Pakistan, up until the ascent to power by General Zia ul-Haq in 1977.

We then elaborate on the Islamization program of the Zia government itself. This program affects social, political, and economic institutions, and breaks down into four areas: economic policies, judicial reforms, the introduction of an Islamic penal code, and a new educational policy. It is the effects of this Islamization program on various dimensions of social life that following chapters will analyze and critique.

FOUNDATIONS OF POLITICAL AUTHORITY

Foundations of political authority in Islam can be traced back to the early community established by the Prophet Muhammad in Mecca. As elaborated at that time, the purpose of the state was to enforce the divine law, as revealed in the Qur'an (the Word of God as revealed to Muhammad) and sunnah (the practice of the Prophet Muhammad). Together, they were seen as containing God's dictates on what man should be and do, and as showing a segment of God's plan for creation. However, it was believed that an individual alone could not conform entirely to the injunctions of Islam unless and until the practical affairs of his society were in line with God's revealed plan.

Two sciences, *tafsir* (Qur'anic commentary) and *fiqh* (jurisprudence), were stressed in the early period of the religion's development.[1] Leonard Binder, writing on Pakistani society during the rule of Ayub Khan, further clarifies the concept of fiqh: "Jurisprudence, fiqh, was the pre-eminent Islamic science. All law is pre-existing and eternal. Right and wrong are known by revelation (the Qur'an) and through reports handed down by tradition of the sayings and doings of the Prophet *(hadith)* (Binder 1963:23).

However, as Goldziher (1981:55) observes, the early scholars of fiqh did not intend to "embitter the life of the Muslin by imprisoning him in a stockade of legal restraint." The *niyya* (intent of the law) is fundamental to its validity. The spirit behind Islam—to obey God's laws in accordance with the shari'a—must never be forgotten when passing or enforcing any law.[2]

Ibn Khaldun, the great classical Islamic theorist, elaborated on the relationship between the state and religious society in his well-known *Al-Muqaddima*. Basing his observations on the roles which the Prophet and the Rashidun Caliphate[3] played in defending and spreading the Islamic religion, he suggests three elements which are critical in the creation and institutionalization of an Islamic state:

1. *Asabiyah* (group feeling), the propensity for cohesion and therefore segmentation;
2. The emergence of a ruling structure which assumes leadership functions;
3. A large community *(umma)* based on religion.

The state is defined primarily in terms of its capacity to maintain justice and to defend the Muslim religion.[4] If the state fails to enforce the divine law, the believer still remains under the obligation to observe the law (Khadduri 1955:24). The Amir (e.g., ruler, king, or caliph) is given authority in the shari'a to do whatever is necessary to enforce the law and provide for the well-being of his citizenry. However, the Amir does not rule alone; he must consult *(mushwarat)* with others who are concerned with the affairs of the state (Ahmad 1975:144). Responsibility lies equally with the ruler and his counselors, but no decision that conflicts with divine law or the traditions of the Prophet may be upheld. The Qur'an is very clear on this point: "Obedience is obligatory until the ruler orders the commission of a sinful act. Those, who would accept their [rulers'] falsehood as Truth, and help them in tyranny and oppression, have no relation to the Prophet. . . . In case the Amir violates the shari'a, the *millat* [community] is released of its allegiance to the Amir" (quoted in Ahmad 1975:161).

All penalties in Islamic law conform to two categories: punishment of crimes against religious and military discipline, and penalties relating to private vengeance (Schacht 1964:175). Three types of penalties exist: *hadd* (pl. *hudud*), *ta'zir* (pl. *ta'azir*) and *qisa* (pl. *qisas*). These differ not only in severity and justification but in philosophy as well. Hudud crimes are regarded as being against God's commands, and are consequently normative and absolute (Kara 1977:139). Therefore, hudud punishments, the severest category (which forms the basis of the Islamic penal code in contemporary Pakistan), are meted out for the violation or neglect of any divinely ordained command. Crimes for which these punishments may apply include theft, adultery/fornication, the consumption of alcohol, slander, robbery, and apostasy. Hudud punishments apply under specific circumstances with specific evidence of the crime. Ta'azir punishments are for other, lesser wrong acts. These punishments are left to the discretion of the community leaders. Qisas concern laws of retaliation; though drafts have been forwarded twice to the Federal Council by the Council of Islamic Ideology, qisas have not yet been incorporated into Pakistan's legal code.

Prescribed sources of revenue (and sanctioned donations) are also important in Islam. There are two categories: religious revenue, which is collected only from Muslims; and secular revenue, collected mostly from non-Muslims. Of the thirteen sources of revenue, the ones which apply to contemporary Pakistan include zakat (a tax of 2½ percent paid annually on total worth of assets); 'ushr (a tax on a Muslim's agricultural lands); *sadqat* (unfixed alms offered occasionally by Muslims); and *waqf* (endowments for religious institutions) (Ahmad 1975:228–29). The chapters by Ann Mayer and Grace Clark address in detail the issue of taxation along Islamic lines in Pakistan.

THE HISTORICAL DEBATE IN SOUTH ASIA

During its tenure, the Mughal state was constantly searching for a durable base for stability, since four-fifths of its subjects were non-Muslims.[5] Though administration and revenue collection were conducted according to classical Islamic tenets, no satisfactory basis for governing the country could be found within Islamic law as it had originally been codified (Faruki 1971:86). Therefore, when the Indian economy was later transformed by colonialism, other social institutions necessarily underwent profound changes resulting from the newly superimposed structures. When the British organized the *zamindari* and *ryotwari* taxation systems, Western laws were imposed which enabled these systems to function. In time, contracts had to be signed, districts had to be ruled, criminals had to be punished; except in the sphere of family law, British law was unilaterally imposed wherever the British Raj extended. A clearly defined separation between religion and the state emerged, underscored by the presence of secular non-Muslim foreign rulers. The Muslim community became essentially powerless against the British throughout most of the nineteenth century.

During this period, however, the Hindu community was experiencing a revitalization. Religious leaders promoting the "rediscovery" of classical Hindu culture (such as Roy and Tagore) were soon followed by secularizing "moderates" (deBary 1958:109) promoting nationalism, social progress, and economic improvement. The British contributed to this revival by often favoring the Hindu community in sociopolitical affairs. They regarded the Muslims as their political opponents, especially because Muslims had led the unsuccessful revolution of 1857.[6]

Much can be written about the varied historical influences which culminated in the formation of an "Islamic homeland," Pakistan, in the subcontinent. However, the important issue here is to understand the various ideas held by different leaders when they called for a separate state for Muslims.[7] It is this question of interpretation which provides the backdrop against which the present government's Islamic laws are being promulgated. Since the demand for a Muslim state arose, the role Islam should play in its political structure has been a problematic issue.

Note that I am careful not to say that the leaders called for an "Islamic state." That would imply that they intended to adopt Islamic laws and establish some form of a theocratic state based on classical precedent. Most historians claim that Sayyid Ahmad Khan, Mohammad Iqbal, and Mohammad Ali Jinnah, the three men regarded as the major leaders behind the Muslim nationalist movement, were clear on this point: they wanted to establish a secular state, but one in which Muslims would not be dominated by any other group, especially by the Hindus. Islam was used as "a motivating force to rally the Muslims to the cause of Pakistan politically" (Hasan 1980:3), but the resulting state was to be secular in structure.

At this point, I will introduce the main characters in the drama, and leave it to Hamza Alavi in the following chapter to elaborate on their differing compositions, ideologies, and stances.

Sir Sayyid Ahmad Khan organized a socio-educational revival movement in the late 1800s. He argued that Muslims were suffering under the British Raj because they refused to participate in British institutions in India, particularly in educational institutions. Social and educational advancement was imperative if Muslims hoped to achieve power. In 1877, Sayyid Ahmad Khan founded the Muhammadan Anglo-Oriental (MAO) College at Aligarh, which emphasized scientific knowledge and Western philosophy, with minimal religious training. Three years later, he developed a traveling "Muhammadan Educational Conference" which held meetings in various cities in northern India, spreading the message of what had now become known as the Aligarh movement, namely that emancipation for Muslims in India lay in their getting a modern education.

Sir Sayyid Ahmad Khan is credited as the founder of the two-nations theory. Loyal to the British in India, he nonetheless argued that there were two nations (Hindu and Muslim) living together in the subcontinent, each with its own culture, history, society, and customs. The two-nations theory, further elaborated by Iqbal, Jinnah, and others, became the legitimating concept behind the later demand for Pakistan.[8]

In 1906, the Agha Khan led an elite delegation of predominantly Aligarh-educated Muslims, the future Muslim League, to the British viceroy's summer retreat in Simla. They wanted to ensure that the Muslims received a fair share of the proposed constitutional reforms. Lord Minto was sympathetic to their demands, and when the reforms were enacted in 1909, the league was successful in achieving separate representation for Muslims in most provinces. However, it was still an elite organization, composed of rural landlords and the lesser Muslim bourgeoisie. It was not the *'ulema* (religious leaders) who began to organize for an independent Muslim state, but rather the more secularized classes. Not until Allama Iqbal's writings became the inspiration for the political movement was a bridge provided which finally transformed the Muslim League into a mass-based movement in the early 1940s.

Even Jinnah, considered the Father of the Nation, probably did not intend to form a theocratic state, nor did he envision a mass migration in which all Hindus and Sikhs would leave the new state. Initially, he just wanted to safeguard Muslims' rights in an independent India. As late as 1939, long after having been chosen by Iqbal to lead the Muslim League following the Round Table conference in 1931, he is said to have told a small delegation of pro-Pakistan students from Cambridge, "I am getting more and more convinced that you are right in spite of myself."

At the conference in Lahore, which resulted in the Lahore Resolution of 1940 calling for an independent Pakistan, Jinnah argued that since the northeast and northwest areas of the subcontinent were inhabited mostly by Muslims, these areas should become a separate state. Jinnah envisioned a modern, progressive, Western-oriented country where religious minorities would enjoy the same rights and privileges as Muslims. In his inaugural address as Pakistan's first president in August 1947, Jinnah said that questions of religion and religiosity would diminish, and that "in course of time Hindus would cease to be Hindus and Muslims would cease to be Muslims, not in the religious sense, because that is the personal faith of each individual, but in the political sense as citizens of the State." (quoted in Naim 1979:213).

Followers of the Aligarh movement and of Jinnah have often been referred to as modernists, for they draw on Western culture for its legal codes, industrial modes, and social norms. These Westernized Muslims accept a demarcation between religious and political life, that is, they support the notion of a secular state.[9] This is a modern conception in that traditional Muslim society does not divide up into such separate institutional spheres (Gellner 1981).

However, many religious leaders during the Independence struggle did not subscribe to the secularizing philosophies of the Aligarh movement and the Muslim League. The two most prominent groups were the Deobandis and the Jamiat-i-ulema-i-Hind.

The Deoband School was founded by Muhammad Qasim Nanawtawi in the mid–1800s. Noted for its orthodox theological scholarship, this religious institute became the antithesis of Aligarh. It completely disassociated itself from Western education, specializing instead in Islamic traditional sciences. The movement's leaders, the 'ulema, were politically hostile towards the British and purportedly supported the 1857 Rebellion. However, most of the Deobandis did not support the demand for a separate Muslim state. Instead, they claimed that as Islam was a universal religion, it could not be said to be confined within national borders.[10]

In the wake of the Khilafat movement in 1919, some of the 'ulema affiliated with the Deobandi *madrasa* were among those who founded a religious/political movement, the Jamiat-i-ulema-i-Hind. They believed in a composite form of Indian nationalism; opposing the British in India, they were nonetheless against the idea of a separate Muslim state. At partition, this group split, with the new Jamiat-i-ulema-i-Islam supporting Pakistan, while many adherents of both the Deoband School and the Jamiat-i-ulema-i-Hind remained in India.

As a direct response to the Lahore Resolution, Maulana Maududi formed a new group in 1941, the Jama'at-i-Islami. Its purpose was the creation of a disciplined, morally upright, ideological body which would become the agent of an Islamic revolution in Indian society (Ahmad and Von Grunebaum 1970:20). Maududi argued that an Islamic revival would in fact dissipate Hindu-Muslim conflict, and that there was no need for the Muslims to separate themselves from the Hindus. It must be noted that this stance was not a traditional one, but rather a dynamic response to current political events. Maududi's group, however, had been located in eastern Punjab in 1947; due to anti-Muslim sentiment in that area, they had to migrate to Pakistan. The Jama'at soon evolved into a political party, demanding the establishment of an Islamic state in Pakistan. The group was the first to seek to redefine tradition in the context of the new state.

These movements, although advocating discordant goals, each sought to mobilize Indian Muslims to reach aims which were neither originally nor ostensibly political (Minault 1982:9). The movements promoted greater Muslim self-awareness and, in doing so, shaped the conflict which ultimately arose between those promoting a Muslim-led secular state and those demanding an Islamic state.

Initially, questions of national identity and ideology were overshadowed by the more basic problems of Pakistan's national survival. In the thiry years since partition, however, Islamic principles have increasingly been included in the state's political apparatus, while the slogan "Islam in Danger" has solidified public sentiment behind the state when it saw its stability threatened (e.g., in the wars with India, and when faced with internal dissent in Bengal and Baluchistan).

The first major occasion where this conflict over the role of Islam in the state emerged was the anti-Ahmadiya riots of 1953. The government's response to the 'ulema's unsuccessful demands that the Ahmadiyas be declared a minority was decisive: martial law was imposed.[11] However, important questions concerning the nature of an Islamic state and who should participate in it were raised. Subsequently, the first Constitution in 1956 recognized freedom of religion, the right to refuse religious instruction, and the right to practice the religion of one's choice. The promotion of Islamic values was advised in the Directive Principles section, and a repugnancy provision (Article 198: "that no law shall be enacted which is repugnant to the injunctions of Islam") was included. However, the succeeding military regime of Ayub Khan was clearly secular; not only were no shari'a-based laws enacted, but the state's attention was focused on its relationship with the international capitalist system and, through its Basic Democracies program, on gaining some degree of political legitimacy from the West.

The preamble to the 1962 Constitution proclaimed the sovereignty of Almighty Allah over the entire universe and stated that Pakistan was based on "Islamic principles of social justice." Although Pakistan was officially declared an "Islamic Republic," no elements of classical fiqh were included. In effect, it was an Islamic republic in name only. Ayub Khan's priorities lay in other areas of Pakistan's development, such as industrial growth. His approach to Islam was consistent with that of the majority of Pakistanis—not to participate in activities repugnant to the religion—and his government reflected that position. However, subsequent events (land reforms, industrial growth, the 1965 war, and the Tashkent agreement over Kashmir) caused the dissension between those advocating a secular state and those supporting an Islamic state to resurface during the regime of Zulfikar Ali Bhutto.

After the ravaging civil war of 1971, when East Bengal achieved its independence and Bhutto became Pakistan's populist prime minister, the government began a program designed to incorporate certain Islamic concepts into the state's structure. Bhutto and his Pakistan People's Party used the rallying cry of "Islamic socialism" in appealing to the masses. The identity of the state was clearly Islamic, while its ideology was to be socialist. Pakistan, whose very being had been questioned in 1971, could now assert its raison d'être.

The 1973 Constitution declared Pakistan to be a parliamentary republic (it had previously been a presidential republic with a strong-arm head of state) and, for the first time, proclaimed Islam as the state religion. In addition, the following articles were included:

> Article 31 (clause 1): The policy of the state is to try to help Muslims live in accordance with the fundamental principles of Islam;
>
> Article 31 (clause 2): Qur'anic instruction is compulsory for all Muslims;

> Article 227: All the existing laws are to be brought into conformity with the injunctions of Islam;
>
> Article 228: A Council of Islamic Ideology is instituted [to inform and help enforce Article 227]. (Gankovsky and Moskalenko 1978:143)

While Ayub Khan's constituency consisted of the expanding industrial class, Bhutto's constitutency included the landed rural classes (from which he came) and the laboring classes. Bhutto adopted Islamic slogans, particularly those stressing egalitarianism and social justice (Esposito 1980:149), as a means of legitimating his economic policies, thereby increasing his popularity. However, the Pakistan People's Party government focused its efforts on liberal policies including labor benefits, nationalizations, and rural land reforms. There was no attempt to include specific Islamic laws in the legal system until it became politically expedient to do so in early 1977 (Sayeed 1980; Burki 1980), when drinking, gambling, and night clubs were banned. This was soon followed by the replacement of Friday for Sunday as the weekly holiday.

There was a contradiction in Bhutto's policies, however. It was not in his advocacy of a socialist interpretation of Islamic ideology; such an interpretation, as Maxime Rodinson (1978) and the Libyan experience have shown, is conceivable. Rather, the contradiction rested in Bhutto's vocal support of socialism on the one hand, and his maintenance of both feudal and capitalist social institutions on the other. Pakistan had no socialist revolution under Bhutto; he made a number of promises to the working classes which he never intended to keep.[12] Bhutto's nationalization of factories provides an example of this contradiction. In other countries, workers have recognized and assumed responsibility for running factories as the result of organized mass movements. In Pakistan, Bhutto nationalized factories to expedite his centralization of power through political patronage, at a time when workers were ill-prepared to take control. Bhutto clung to the slogan of "Islamic socialism," intending it to be so ambiguous that he could not be criticized by either section of his constituency.

In January 1977, Bhutto announced that national elections would be held two months later. Nine opposition parties formed a coalition virtually overnight, the Pakistan National Alliance (PNA). Although parties advocating religious orthodoxy (e.g., the Jama'at-i-Islami and the Jamiat-i-ulema-i-Islam) as well as secular ones (e.g., the National Democratic Party and Tehrik-i-Istiqlal) constituted the PNA, its unifying claim to legitimacy and viability was its demand that a firm system of Islamic laws be incorporated into the state apparatus. The PNA declared that the Bhutto government had not followed Islamic principles and was therefore illegitimate. Though not all members of the Pakistan National Alliance envisioned similar outcomes of the movement, they all tried to portray the movement as both "Islamic" and "just."

The Pakistan People's Party government enjoyed an overwhelming victory over the PNA in the March elections. Immediately, charges of election fraud and tampering were leveled against the government. Popular protests broke out, demanding the government's resignation. Civil order virtually collapsed in the confusion, and as it had done so often before in Pakistan's brief history, the army stepped in. On 5 July 1977, General Zia ul-Haq became the Chief Martial Law Administrator (CMLA) in a bloodless coup d'état.

THE SHIFT TOWARDS ISLAMIC LAWS UNDER THE ZIA GOVERNMENT

The Pakistan National Alliance, particularly the groups rallied around the late Maulana Maududi and Mufti Mahmud, applauded the military's intervention. By invitation, some members soon joined the government as cabinet advisors. Though not elected to office, they were finally in power nonetheless.

So too was General Zia. He promised national elections, but continued to postpone them, finally instituting an indefinite postponement in October 1979, more than two years later.

A major challenge facing the Zia government was one of legitimacy. Now that the army once again had control of state power, it was hesitant to relinquish it. Yet General Zia himself had no legal right to head the state: in secular terms, he was not an elected officeholder; in religious terms, he was head of state neither due to the consent of the people or their leaders (Sunni fiqh) nor as a *mujtahid* who could interpret the law (Shi'a fiqh). But with the support of political parties of the "religious right," he claimed that his government would finally put Pakistan on its destined path. Zia and his supporters reiterated that Pakistan's raison d'être was the establishment of an Islamic state.

Concomitantly, leaders of the political opposition were imprisoned or harassed. Members of the Bhutto family were put under house arrest, while Bhutto himself was charged—and ultimately executed—as an accomplice in an earlier political assassination.

With his opposition effectively silenced, at least temporarily, General Zia proclaimed himself president and vowed to bring in a new state apparatus based on Islamic law. He stated, in introducing his program of "Nizam-i-Islam" in early 1979: "It is Allah's beneficence that the present government has been able to fulfill these aspirations [introduction of Islamic system in Pakistan] of the people. In the short period of one and a half years, so much work has been done that I am today formally announcing the introduction of the Islamic system in the country. May Allah bless our efforts!" (Zia ul-Haq 1979:3).

Since such a military state has no traditional religious legitimacy, Zia's actions must be viewed as an attempt to redefine tradition. His followers in the *Islam-pasand* parties (favoring Islam playing a more public role in the state) viewed the new government's actions as a reassertion in contemporary times of the possibility—and validity—of rule by Islamic laws, for the basis of a moral society is found within the shari'a.

As stated earlier, the Islamization program of the Zia government can be broken down into four areas: economic programs, judicial reforms, the introduction of an Islamic penal code, and a new educational policy conforming to Islamic tenets. As the chapters by S. J. Burki, Ann Mayer, and Grace Clark address the first area extensively, we will concern ourselves here with only the latter three policies.

The government's program of judicial reforms established shariat benches in the superior courts (Third President's Order, 2/10/79). Three Muslim judges *(qazis)* sit on the shariat benches in each High Court. Their purpose is to "examine and decide the question whether or not any law or provision of law is repugnant to the injunctions of Islam" (Chap. 3A, Article 203B). Any such law immediately becomes void, and should be amended at once, although the decision can be appealed to the Shari'a Appellate Bench of the Supreme Court. A lawyer practicing in front of the shariat bench must have been enrolled as a High Court advocate for at least five years and must also be "an A'lim, who, in the opinion of the High Court, is well-versed in Shariat" (Article 203B, 5–6).[13] Therefore, until recently Pakistan had three coexisting legal systems: civil, martial, and Islamic (shariat).

The establishment of shari'a courts in this manner is interesting largely for what the order did not do. It did not restrict the power of either the civil or military courts operating concurrently in Pakistan, except to ensure that the laws were not repugnant to Islam. Nor was there an overhaul of the legal system, placing all laws into conformity at once. Instead, only when a law was challenged as repugnant to Islamic injunction did a shari'a bench become involved. In addition, the question of legal derivation was not raised; laws were decreed as conforming to Islamic shari'a, but no attempt was made to derive the legal system directly from the shari'a.

However, General Zia apparently became fearful of the power of the shariat benches, for only a year later (and just a month following Bhutto's execution) he revised the amendment, clearly placing the military courts at the top of the legal structure. Although he had previously stated that "the supremacy of Islamic law has been established over the law of the land" (Zia ul-Haq 1979:4), now no court could make any order "relating to the validity or effect of any Martial Law Regulation or Order made by the Chief Martial Law Administrator [Zia] . . . or to the validity or effect of any judgement or sentence passed by a Military Court or Tribunal; or issue any process against the CMLA . . . or a Martial Law Administrator or any person acting under the authority of either" (Article 199, 3A). If the public feels that the president is doing something wrong, they have no legal recourse. They cannot take him to court, because he has placed himself—and the military government—above the Islamic legal system. Military expediency overrides Islamic reassertion.

At the same time, Zia disbanded the system of shariat benches on High Courts and established a Federal Shari'a Court, consisting of five members headquartered in Islamabad, the national capital. Lawyers appearing before the court do not plead for their clients per se, but instead state, expound, and interpret injunctions of Islam relevant to the proceedings.

All judges throughout the legal system had to take a loyalty oath to the president. Quite a few resigned over this issue, although most took the oath.

Interesting too is that traditional clothing is prescribed for the shari'a court jurists. They are to wear black *sherwanis* with a white collar inside, white *shalwars* (pajamas), and black shoes and socks. If headgear is used, it must be a black Quaid cap. This is significant in that it is a highly visible way for the government to combine Islam and nationalism, as the sherwani is popularly considered to be the "national dress." While such traditional dress is occasionally worn by men in nonceremonial settings, pants and shirts have also been popular. A similar code has since been recommended for all high-level civil servants.

The shari'a states that the ruler must govern in consultation with his subjects, and that the Sunnah is to have final authority at all times. The system instituted by the Zia government falls far short of this injunction, for the Chief Martial Law Administrator, his deputies, and the military courts have all been placed above the shari'a courts. By forcing all judges to take a loyalty oath (as well as by maintaining fairly strict press censorship and refusing to hold national elections), General Zia had eliminated popular channels of protest. The Qur'an enjoins the ruler to hold a public meeting weekly, when he can come into contact with his subjects and hear their opinions. It is a way of maintaining both contact and support with the polity, a concept elusive to the present government, which has not initiated this practice.

On 25 January 1983, the government established an ombudsman's office, the *Wafaqi Mohtasib*. The Mohtasib has the same powers of inspection and punishment that are vested in a civil court. He may undertake investigations into any allegation of maladministration on the part of any agency or its employees. The government had come under strong criticism that its own ranks were not adequately policed, and that when a person had a complaint, there was no institutionalized system of recourse, a state of affairs contrary to Islamic provisions.

One problem with the new judicial structure concerns the expertise of lawyers practicing before the shari'a courts. The majority of lawyers conversant with Western law are unfamiliar with Islamic law. A shariat law faculty was established at Islamabad's Quaid-i-azam University in 1979, but other law schools in the country have not followed suit. People who have an inclination to study Western jurisprudence are, by and large, not interested in studying Islamic law, and vice versa. Therefore, it is difficult to find lawyers conversant in both forms of law.

A second problem concerns the richness and complexity of Islamic law. Given all the schools of fiqh which can be relied upon, it is difficult to state with absolute certainty that any given interpretation is in fact the most valid and legally binding.[14]

The final feature of Islamic law adopted by the Pakistan government concerns the new penal code, the enforcement of hudud punishments. These laws provide punishments for three major categories of crime: *saraka* (theft of private property); *zina* (adultery and fornication [and *qazf* (bearing false witness to adultery and fornication)]); and *el-sharab* (the consumption of intoxicants). A series of Islamic punishments were ordained according to the severity of the act, the particular circumstances under which the act is carried out, and whether the act is liable to hudud or ta'azir punishments. A common punishment is lashing, the particulars of which are explained in the Execution of the Punishment of Whipping Ordinance, 1979. A woman may sit while being whipped, while a man must stand. The weather cannot be too hot or too cold, and care is to be taken not to kill or maim the culprit, who must be in good physical health.

In order for a criminal to receive the harsher hadd punishment for a theft, the adult must knowingly and surreptitiously have committed a single theft worth the equivalent of 4.457 grams of gold or more. There must also be an admission of guilt by the thief, along with sworn testimony of two honest, adult, *salah* Muslim men (though not from the victim) who can give eye-witness evidence of the crime. The punishment for a first offense is amputation of the right hand from the joint of the wrist; for a second offense, it is amputation of the left foot to the ankle; for a third offense (or more), the punishment is life imprisonment. However, there are many exceptions to the order, as when a guest steals from his host, a worker from his employer, or when the thief's left hand or right foot is missing or not usable.[15] If an adult attacks another person with the intent to commit robbery *(haraabah),* and admits to the crime and there are witnesses, the following punishments apply:

a) If neither a murder nor a theft was actually committed, the accused may receive a maximum of thirty lashes and rigorous imprisonment for a minimum of three years;
b) If a theft is committed but not murder, the punishment for theft applies;
c) If a murder is committed, the punishment is execution.

Seemingly a holdover from a previous law, the punishment for anyone aiding a cattle theft for a share of the booty is rigorous imprisonment for a maximum of fourteen years or a maximum of seventy lashes, along with a fine and confiscation of all his immovable property. If a person attempts to commit any crime covered by this ordinance and is unsuccessful, he is subject to a maximum imprisonment of ten years.

As well as introducing hudud punishments for theft, the government instituted another safeguard of private property through its Islamization program. Citing indiscriminate nationalizations and other economic policies of the Bhutto government "responsible for the wrecking of the national economy," the constitution was amended, guaranteeing "that in future, no industrial concern would be nationalized without appropriate compensation" (Zia ul-Haq 1979:16).

Zina offences, concerning crimes of adultery and fornication, are highly circumscribed, as are charges of false accusations of zina (qazf). There is no legal difference between the punishment for rape and the punishment for other forms of zina offenses. If the accused is a virgin or is married, the penalty is death by stoning; if unmarried (e.g., widowed, divorced, a prostitute), the penalty is one hundred lashes.

As in the private property statute, the necessary proof for zina is a confession, but in this case, four adult male eye-witnesses are necessary for the harsher hudud sentence. There are so many exceptions to this law—and the chances of such an act being committed in front of four eye-witnesses are so scant—that as of this date, there have been no known deaths by stoning and few whippings for this offense. The government has resorted to the latter punishment only in cases of rape or when a woman has deserted her husband. In effect, the conservative view of "woman as property" has been upheld by this law.

Although Bhutto, in his last year in power, outlawed bars and nightclubs, the present government has far surpassed those restrictions in its enforcement of prohibition, enacted by decree on 10 February 1979. Anyone who imports, transports, manufactures, processes, sells, or allows consumption of an intoxicant on his premises may be liable for a maximum of five years imprisonment, thirty lashes, and a fine. For simply possessing an intoxicant, the punishment is two years imprisonment or thirty lashes, and a fine.

Any adult Muslim found drinking alcohol is liable to the hadd punishment of eighty lashes (again, a confession is required as well as the eye-witness testimony of two adults). If the proof is insufficient, then the ta'zir punishment of three years imprisonment and/or thirty lashes applies.

The ta'zir punishment also applies to non-Muslim Pakistani citizens found drinking alcohol except as part of a religious ritual, and to a non-Muslim foreigner found drinking alcohol in a public place.

The new educational policy is the only one of the four areas of Zia's Islamization program not directly based on Qur'anic injunction; it relates instead to the assimilation and acceptance of the government's Islamization program among the people. The administration intended that the new educational policy of revising textbooks and course curricula to conform to Islamic values (e.g., establishing separate educational facilities for males and females; making religious education compulsory for Muslims; and making Urdu the language of instruction in schools) be an affirmation of its commitment to Islam. The traditional schools of Islamic education have also been affected by the new policy as secular subjects have been introduced into their course curricula. As noted earlier, a shariat faculty was set up at Quaid-e-azam University in 1979. A year later, it became a separate institution, the Islamic University. Carroll (1982:74) contends that the government's objective was the creation of an integrated system of education bridging the bifurcation between the traditional/religious and the modern/scientific streams.

Recent events in Pakistan serve to underscore the vastly differing opinions on the government's Islamization efforts. The government held a national referendum on 19 December 1984 on its Islamization program. The scope of the referendum was limited in that it did not question specific points nor revive the issue of *ijtihad*. Rather, it simply stated that if the people of Pakistan felt the government was doing a good job of Islamicizing the various social institutions in the state, then the government would remain in power for an additional five years. Opposition groups had already been outlawed and were not allowed to participate. Anyone found boycotting the referendum was not to be permitted to contest any election for seven years; anyone advocating that others boycott the referendum was to be imprisoned for five years. There were rumors of demonstrations throughout the country in opposition to the referendum, yet on the day following it, the government claimed a 97.7 percent approval vote, with 62 percent of the thirty-five million registered voters casting ballots.

The government then announced that with this backing, it would proceed with a program to eliminate all forms of non-Islamic banking by 1 January 1985, and to ensure that the economy be in conformity with Islam by June 1985.

On 24 February 1985, for the first time since 1977, elections were held for the national and provincial assemblies. The opposition, as expected, called for a boycott of this election as well. The government claimed a victory in that 50 percent of registered voters were said to have participated, even though some of the government's supporters did not win their seats. The meaning of this outcome, at the time of this writing, remains unclear, as General Zia has not said what responsibilities the members of the assemblies will have. One thing is certain: power will remain vested in the executive branch.

The dilemma for opponents of the government's Islamization policies is that the new laws apparently serve purposes other than simply religious ones. It has become politically expedient to advocate a "return to the Islamic path" since to come out against such a slogan would result in being cast as an "enemy of Islam." Opposition to these laws is a stance not permitted in Islam. Thus those opposing the enactment of the new laws have had a difficult time articulating the subtle distinction between their appreciation of classical Islamic law and their criticism of those laws recently adopted by the state. They argue that most of the new laws are punishment-related; while the new laws embrace the restrictions of Islam, they fail to capture its spirit.

The government has asserted that it will restore democracy in Pakistan within an Islamic framework. President Zia ul-Haq lifted martial law and vowed to allow political activity on 31 December 1985. However, a number of restrictions have been placed on that participation, such as a bill which bans members of national and provincial parliaments from switching parties without seeking reelection, and which requires political parties to register with the country's electoral commission after having proven that they are committed to Islamic ideology. It will be the Zia government, despite Junejo's presence as prime minister, which will determine if a party qualifies as sufficiently "committed" or not. Needless to say, it is highly doubtful that the main opposition party, the Pakistan People's Party, will ever be deemed to be so qualified.[16]

In effect, it appears from the slowly unfolding programs of Islamic prohibitions and punishments, economic measures, and restrictions on political activities introduced by the current government, that it is unlikely that the government truly intends to increase viable public participation in the political process. However, we must not lose sight of the fact that this has never been as important to the present government as its stated objective of bringing Pakistani society and polity into conformity with Islamic principles. How it has fared on this score is left to the following chapters for analysis.

NOTES

1. Four Sunni schools of thought have survived. Malikite fiqh has been popular in Egypt, North Africa, and Spain. It permits the principle of *ijma* (collective reasoning), but only as an extension of the Qur'an and hadith. The Hanafi school, which became the most widespread and which is dominant in South Asia, allows for the introduction of *qiyas* (analogical deduction) as well as ijma. Shafi fiqh, popular in parts of the Levant and in pre-Shi'a Iran, restricts the appliation of qiyas by a more extended application of hadith. Hanbali fiqh, which provides the basis of Wah'habism, found in Saudi Arabia, opposes the use of both ijma and qiyas, arguing that man-made interpretations are fallible.

The jurisprudence of Shi'ism, fiqh Jaf'aria, does not regard the era of ijtihad (interpretation) as having closed, as do the four Sunni schools. There are many substantive differences between Sunni and Shi'a law, including those laws pertaining to punishments and revenue collection. These differences form a basis for the objections by Shi'as in contemporary Pakistan to the imposition of Sunni laws on the Shi'a community.

2. For further elaboration on basic concepts of Islamic law, see Joseph Schact, *Introduction to Islamic Law* (1964), especially pages 116–211; and Ignaz Goldziher, *Introduction to Islamic Theology and Law* (1981), particularly pages 31–66 and 230–67. Asaf Fyzee, *Outlines of Muhammadan Law* (London: Oxford University Press, 1964), delineates how the British interpreted Islamic law in South Asia.

3. The Rashidun Caliphate, according to Sunni Islam, are the four political successors to the Prophet: Abu Bakr, Omar, Usman, and 'Ali. They are considered to have

been the Prophet's companions, were selected by the community in succession, and ruled according to legitimate precepts. Shi'as, however, regard only 'Ali's succession as valid. He is considered the first imam in an inherited line of twelve. For further elaboration on the laws of Sunni succession, see Kemal A. Faruki, *The Evolution of Islamic Constitutional Theory and Practice from 610 to 1926* (1971); for Shi'a succession see 'Allamah Sayyid Muhammad Husayn Tabataba'i, *Shi'ite Islam*, trans. and ed. Seyyed Hossein Nasr (Albany: State University of New York Press, 1975).

Reinhard Bendix, in exploring sacred and secular foundations of political authority, presents an interesting argument in his *Kings or People: Power and the Mandate to Rule* (Berkeley: University of California Press, 1980). He contends that the fact that the Rashidun Caliphate was based on election sets a precedent legitimating participatory democracy in Sunni states. The *imamate*, on the other hand, provides the foundation for monarchies, or inherited forms of rule, in Shi'a states.

4. This statement is simplistic, but any brief analysis distorts the true concept. For a succinct discussion of the Traditionalist's view of the state, see Maulana Abul Ala Maududi, *Islamic Law and Constitution* (Lahore: Islamic Publications, n.d.). The contradictory Modernist interpretation is seen in Fazlur Rahman, "Implementation of the Islamic Concept of State in the Pakistani Milieu," *Islamic Studies* 6 (1967): 205–24.

5. The dilemma of the Mughals differed greatly from the situation of the Ottoman Caliphate. Only *dhimmis* (*el-e-kitab*, people of the book), Jews and Christians, who made up the Turkish minority, had a protected legal status under Islamic law. Indian non-Muslims were predominantly Hindus *(kafirs)* who were not protected under such law (although Hindus were de facto treated as el-e-kitab).

6. Allama Iqbal's famous poem "Shikwa and Jawab-i-Shikwa" ("Complaint and Answer," trans. Altaf Husain [4th ed., Karachi: Pakistan Herald Press, 1966]) gives a sense of the sociopolitical constraints faced by Indian Muslims under the British.

7. Ahmad and Von Grunebaum (1970) have compiled writings from all perspectives of modern South Asian Islamic thought. Their bibliographic study is especially valuable, presenting an overview of the major actors participating in the historical dissonance.

8. For a succinct elaboration of the two-nations theory, including a lucid discussion of Muslim nationalism in the subcontinent and the demand for a separate state, see Manzooruddin Ahmed, "Iqbal and Jinnah on the 'Two Nations' Theory" (in Naim 1979:41–76). For further historical analysis of this time period, see A. H. Alberuni, *Makers of Pakistan and Modern Muslim India* (Lahore: Ashraf, 1950) and J. M. S. Baljon, Jr., *The Reforms and Religious Ideas of Sir Sayyid Ahmad Khan* (3rd rev. ed., Lahore: Ashraf, 1964).

9. Fazlur Rahman (1982) expands on this notion of Islamic modernism, tracing its historical development and elaborating on its contemporary forms.

10. For more information on the Deoband movement, see Ziya-ul-Hasan Faruqi, *The Deoband School and The Demand for Pakistan* (Bombay: Asia Publishing House, 1963); and Barbara D. Metcalf, *Islamic Revival in British India* (Princeton: Princeton University Press, 1982).

11. Khalid bin Sayeed (1980:36–39) presents a good account of the events surrounding the 1953 anti-Ahmadiya riots and the resultant Munir Report. Bowing to political pressure, Bhutto declared the Ahmadiyas to be a non-Muslim minority in 1974.

12. For a general discussion of the Bhutto years, consult Burki (1980). For an elaboration of specific economic policies and their contradictory effects, see Weiss (1983).

13. Lucy Carroll (1982) gives an extensive, detailed account and analysis of the ways in which the Zia government has established the shariat court system.

14. Lucy Carroll (1982:63) retells an interesting account of just such a dilemma which came under Islamic judicial review in 1978, though under the civil court system. Instead of reinterpreting a Hanafi position concerning a marital issue, the court adopted the Shafi and Shi'a interpretations.

15. Shi'a and Sunni jurisprudence also differ somewhat on the manner in which punishments are to be carried out. For example, Sunnis cut off the entire left hand above the wrist in theft cases; Shi'as cut off only the fingers, claiming that the palm is needed to place on the ground while saying one's prayers.

REFERENCES

Ahmad, Aziz, and G.E. Von Grunebaum, eds. 1970. *Muslim Self-Statment in India and Pakistan:1857–1968*. Wiesbaden: Otto Harrassowitz.

Ahmad, Mohammad Aziz. 1975. *The Nature of Islamic Political Theory*. Karachi: Ma'aref.

Ayoob, Mohammed. 1979. "Two Faces of Political Islam: Iran and Pakistan Compared." *Asian Survey* 19, No. 6: 535–46.

Binder, Leonard. 1963. *Religion and Politics in Pakistan*. Berkeley and Los Angeles: University of California Press.

Burki, Shahid Javed. 1980. *Pakistan under Bhutto, 1971–1977*. London: Macmillan.

Carroll, Lucy. 1982. "Nizam-i-Islam: Processes and Conflicts in Pakistan's Programme of Islamisation, with Special Reference to the Position of Women." *Journal of Commonwealth and Comparative Politics* 20: 57–95.

Coulson, N. J. 1964. *A History of Islamic Law*. Islamic Surveys, No. 2. Edinburgh: Edinburgh University Press.

deBary, William Theodore. 1958. *Sources of Indian Tradition* Vol. 2. New York: Columbia University Press.

Donohue, John J. and John L. Esposito, eds. 1982. *Islam in Transition: Muslim Perspectives:* Oxford University Press.

Esposito, John L., ed. 1980. *Islam and Development: Religion and Sociopolitical Change*. Syracuse: Syracuse University Press.

———. 1983. *Voices of Resurgent Islam*. New York: Oxford University Press.

Faruki, Kemal A. 1971. *The Evolution of Islamic Constitutional Theory and Practice from 610 to 1926*. Karachi: National Publishing House.

Gankovsky, Y. V. and V. N. Moskalenko. 1978. *The Three Constitutions of Pakistan*. Lahore: People's Publishing House.

Gellner, Ernest. 1981. *Muslim Society*. Cambridge: Cambridge University Press.

Goldziher, Ignaz. 1981. *Introduction to Islamic Theology and Law*. Translated by Andras and Ruth Hamori. Princeton: Princeton University Press.

Government of Pakistan. 1979. *Islamic Laws (Enforcement of Nizam-E-Mustafa).*

Lahore: Lahore Law Times Publications.

———. 1982. *New Islamic Criminal Laws.* Lahore: Lahore Law Times Publications.

———. Ministry of Law and Parliamentary Affairs. 1980. *The Pakistan Penal Code, 1860 (As Modified up to 3rd February, 1980).* Karachi: Manager of Publications.

Hasan, Masudul. 1980 (?). *Pakistan: The Call of Islam.* Islamabad: Pakistan Publications.

Hassan, Farooq. 1981. *The Concept of State and Law in Islam.* Washington, D.C.: University Press of America.

Ibn Khaldun. 1967. *The Muqaddimah: An Introduction to History.* 2d ed. Translated by Franz Rosenthal. Princeton: Princeton University Press.

Kara, Mustafa A. 1977. "The Philosophy of Punishment in Islamic Law." Ph.d. dissertation, Claremont Graduate School.

Khadduri, Majid. 1955. *War and Peace in the Law of Islam.* Baltimore: Johns Hopkins Press.

Minault, Gail. 1982. *The Khilafat Movement: Religious Symbolism and Political Mobilization in India.* New York: Columbia University Press.

Naim, C. M., ed. 1979. *Iqbal, Jinnah and Pakistan: The Vision and the Reality.* Foreign and Comparative Studies/South Asian Series, no. 5. Syracuse: Maxwell School of Citizenship and Public Affairs, Syracuse University.

Rahman, Fazlur. 1982. *Islam and Modernity: Transformation of an Intellectual Tradition.* Chicago: University of Chicago Press.

Richter, William L. 1979. "The Political Dynamics of Islamic Resurgence in Pakistan." *Asian Survey* 19, No. 6 (June): 547–57.

Rodinson, Maxime. 1978. *Islam and Capitalism.* Translated by Brian Pearce. Austin: University of Texas Press.

Sayeed, Khalid bin. 1980. *Politics in Pakistan: The Nature and Direction of Change.* New York: Praeger Publishers.

Schact, Joseph. 1964. *Introduction to Islamic Law.* Oxford: Oxford University Press.

Stoddard, Philip H., David C. Cuthell, and Margaret W. Sullivan, eds. 1981. *Change and the Muslim World.* Syracuse: Syracuse University Press.

Turner, Bryan S. 1974. *Weber and Islam: A Critical Study.* London: Routledge and Kegan Paul.

Voll, John Obert. 1982. *Islam: Continuity and Change in the Modern World.* Boulder: Westview Press.

Weiss, Anita M. 1983. "The Emergence of an Industrial Bourgeoisie in Punjab, Pakistan: Case Studies of Three Industries." Ph.D. dissertation, Department of Sociology, University of California at Berkeley.

Zafar, Emmanuel. 1981. *Law and Practice of Islamic Hudood.* 1981 edition. Lahore: Khyber Law Publishers.

Zia ul-Haq, Mohammad. 1979. "Introduction of Islamic Laws: Address to the Nation." Islamabad, 10 February.

2

Ethnicity, Muslim Society, and the Pakistan Ideology

Hamza Alavi

There is a pervasive belief, held more widely outside Pakistan than in the country, that Pakistan, like Israel and Iran, is one of three confessional states in the world; that, like Israel, its very origin was to fulfill a religious ideal, to create an Islamic state and Islamic society for the Muslims of India. The regime of General Zia ul-Haq has declared likewise that Pakistan was created to establish an Islamic state for the Muslims of India. Lacking a popular mandate, the military regime has sought its claim to legitimacy, if not its purpose, in divine ordinance.

The irony of the argument that Pakistan was founded on religious ideology lies in the fact that practically every Muslim group and organization in the Indian subcontinent that was specifically religious—Islamic—was hostile to Jinnah and the Muslim League, and strongly opposed the Pakistan movement. A great deal of effort was devoted by Muslim League leaders to winning over the 'ulema. Eventually they succeeded in doing so, but only partially, and only when the creation of Pakistan was just over the horizon.

A claim that Pakistan was created to fulfill the millenarian religious aspirations of Indian Muslims is therefore contradicted by the fact that the principal bearers of the Islamic religion in India were alienated from the Pakistan movement. Conversely, the English-educated leaders of the Pakistan movement, not least Jinnah himself, were committed to secular politics. It is only in retrospect, when history is being rewritten, that Jinnah is pictured as a religious bigot. The fact remains that Islam was not at the center of Muslim nationalism in India, but was brought into the political debate in Pakistan after the nation was created. Its role in the postcolonial period therefore needs to be explained with reference to the political needs of Pakistan's rulers.[1] But instead of undertaking such an analysis, scholars have taken the place of Islam in Pakistan society and politics at face value, echoing the political rhetoric of Pakistani politicians and rulers. This tendency to misconceive the ideological scene in Pakistan is even more pronounced today, when too many scholars have been mesmerized by the growing specter of militant fundamentalist Islam throughout the Muslim world.[2]

In a nutshell, the argument of this paper is that the Pakistan movement was not a movement of Islam but of Muslims. It was not a millenarian movement seeking a divinely ordained political and social system. Rather, it was a movement in which diverse Muslim ethnic groups from different regions of India, representing different social strata and interests, at the center of whom were the emerging Muslim *salariat* (see below), were allied in pursuit of quite material objectives. The alliance, such as it was, did not include all Muslims of India all the time. There was no automatic and universal translation of the attribute of *Muslim by faith* or *Muslim by descent* to an automatic assertion of Muslim ethnic identity. Private affirmation and practice of their faith did not necessarily bring Muslims together into a unified political group. This is demonstrated by the committed noncommunalism of the right-wing Unionist Party, led by Muslims, that dominated Punjab politics, and of the radical Krishak Proja Party, led by A. K. Fazlul Haq, which at various times was the ruling party in Bengal and enjoyed wide support among both Hindus and Muslims of the province.

The Bengal case is particularly apposite for illustrating not only the contingent nature of (Muslim) ethnicity but also the fact that neither Jinnah nor the Muslim League intended to create a state exclusively of Muslims (as against achieving Muslim salariat political power in Muslim majority provinces of India, as they were constituted) or an Islamic state. Faced in May 1947 with the carving up of Bengal between India and Pakistan (which would not be in the interests of the people of Bengal as a whole), influential Muslim as well as Hindu (Congress) leaders of Bengal came together in support of an alternative plan for a united independent Bengal. Bengal Muslim League leader Suhrawardy and some of his colleagues reached an agreement with Congress leaders Sarat Chandra Bose, Kiran Shankar Roy, and others in support of the idea. It is most significant, in the circumstances, that this plan also had Jinnah's full support. After Suhrawardy (on behalf of Bengal leadership) had presented Mountbatten the plan for an independent Bengal side by side with independent India and Pakistan, the latter asked Jinnah what his attitude to such a plan would be. In the record of his interview with Jinnah, Mountbatten wrote: "I asked Mr. Jinnah straight-out what his views were about keeping Bengal united at the price of its remaining out of Pakistan. He said without hesitation, "I would be delighted. What is the use of Bengal without Calcutta. They had much better remain united and independent' " (Mansergh and Moon 1981:452). The plan was vetoed by the Congress High Command, however, and Mountbatten accepted their veto.

Jinnah's unequivocal acceptance of the plan for an independent Bengal shows only too clearly that his aim was not that of bringing together all Muslims of India under a single state at any price. Much less was it that of creating an Islamic state which, arguably, would have been made much easier by the removal of large numbers of non-Muslims by virtue of division of the provinces along communal lines, an option that he did not favor. On the contrary, Jinnah was committed to maintaining the unity of those provinces, even at the price of remaining within a federal Indian union, as his acceptance of the 1946 Cabinet Mission Plan testified. The logic of a federal union solution is best understood if we keep in mind the concerns of Muslims in Muslim minority provinces of India, not least those of Uttar Pradesh (U.P.), who were a central component of the Muslim movement. Their political philosophy was grounded in what one might label the "hostage theory," namely that the fair treatment of Hindu minorities in Muslim majority provinces would be the best guarantee of their own fair treatment by Hindus in independent India. That would not work if Pakistan were exclusively Muslim and even less so if it were a theocratic Islamic state which might invite reciprocal penalties for them in free India.

The movement that ultimately resulted in the creation of Pakistan was comprised of diverse groups, both regionally and socially. Their unity in the political arena was a precarious one. Jinnah's political genius lay precisely in his ability to orchestrate a loose, volatile, and unpredictable coalition of forces. He is generally pictured as a man with a firm and total grip over the groups that he was leading. But that is a myth, made plausible by his powerful and commanding personality. In reality his hold over the various groups was quite tenuous and he had to take them on their own terms. He merely stood at the center of a political process around which diverse regional groups revolved, over whom he had little control.

Jinnah and the All-India Muslim League gave the various regionally-based groups a convenient voice at the center of Indian politics, in discussions with the Indian National Congress and the colonial masters. The landed magnates who ruled over the Muslim majority provinces were prepared to make use of Jinnah and the Muslim League for their own purposes and, to that extent, went along with them. That supported the illusion of a unified Muslim nation in India. But it was a marriage of convenience, for the provincial magnates on whom Jinnah depended for support and for his own legitimacy were not prepared to surrender their local autonomy. It was they who dictated the terms of the alliance, rather than Jinnah and the central Muslim League to whom they were nominally subject. Nevertheless, the idea of a Muslim nation gained temporary currency, and Jinnah became the embodiment of that conception. The Pakistan movement, in that sense and to that extent, became a national movement, on the basis of the two-nations theory that Jinnah propounded, affirming that Muslims of India were a separate nation from Hindus. Insofar as their politics entailed the establishment of their own state, their objective was the creation of a "Muslim state" as a nation state; they did not seek an "Islamic state" as a theocratic conception.

THE MUSLIM SALARIAT

I will argue here that there was one particular social group, more than any other, for whom the conception of Muslim nationhood (rather than religious ideology) was particularly meaningful. That class was a product of the colonial transformation of Indian social structure in the nineteenth century: the class of urban professionals, especially members of the new legal profession. It also included those who had received education that would qualify them for employment as scribes and functionaries in the expanding colonial state apparatus: the men (for few women were so employed) whose instrument of production was the pen. For want of a better term, I have referred to them as the salariat. The term "middle class" is too wide, and "petit bourgeoisie" has connotations, especially in Marxist discourse, that would not refer to this class.

The salariat looms large in colonial societies because there the bulk of the population is rural and agricultural. In the absence of a significant number of people clustered around urban industrial activities, and leaving aside the small number of people engaged in petty trade or in the relatively tiny sector of export trade and finance, the colonial urban society revolved mainly around functionaries of the state, and the educated looked primarily to the government for employment and advancement. It was this class which was at the core of the Indian nationalist movement, demanding a rightful place for Indians in the state apparatus, "Indianization" of services, and the creation of popular institutions of representative government through which they would share in the exercise of power. At the least, they wanted some measure of control over the bureaucracy in the name of "self-government," as distinct from the idea of independence from colonial rule which was not yet on the agenda in the late nineteenth century (McCully 1940; Basu 1974).

The conception of a Muslim nation was articulated most vocally by the Muslim members of the salariat, challenging the slogan of "akhand Bharat" (indivisible India) that was proclaimed by Indian nationalists amongst whom the more advanced and well-established Hindu salariat predominated. In turn, the conception of a unified Muslim Nation of South Asia did not outlast the day of independence and the Partition. On the day that Pakistan was created, Muslim ethnicity had outlived its original purpose. Its goal was realised, but only for the dominant Punjabi component of the Muslim salariat. The interregional coalition of the Muslim salariat broke up. The new privileged group from among them came into focus: the Punjabis (temporarily joined by an elite group of *muhajirs*—Urdu-speaking migrants from India). The Punjabis were preponderant in the bureaucracy and the army and held key positions in the state. They became visible as the new dominant group, winning out over other regional groups who had less than their due share of education, jobs, and power.

The Muslim salariat was not evenly distributed in size and influence in different parts of India. If we take the numbers of persons more than twenty years of age who are literate in English as an index of the size of the salariat, we see the results shown in Table 2.1.

The Muslim salariat of the Punjab was the largest both in terms of its absolute size and in terms of its larger percentage share of the total Punjabi salariat (32 percent). However, even in the Punjab, the share of Muslims in the salariat was smaller relative to Hindus. This was the principal grievance that fueled the Muslim movement in urban Punjab. Since independence, it has been the Punjab salariat that, by virtue of its much greater size and development, occupies a dominant position in the society and the state.

The Urdu-speaking Uttar Pradesh salariat was the next most developed. In contrast to Punjab, the share of Muslims in the Uttar Pradesh salariat was greater than their relative share of the total population. Muslims of Uttar Pradesh had always been a privileged minority, but their

TABLE 2.1

Relative Sizes of Total Muslim Population and Muslim Salariat in India in 1931

POPULATION (IN MILLIONS)	Uttar Pradesh		Punjab		Bengal		Sind	
Total	48.4		28.5		51		3.9	
Muslims	7.2	(15%)	14.9	(52%)	27.8	(54.5%)	2.8	(73%)

LITERATES IN ENGLISH AGED TWENTY YEARS OR MORE	Uttar Pradesh		Punjab		Bengal		Sind	
Total	266,000		185,000		722,435		33,850	
Muslims	49,400	(19%)	58,800	(32%)	175,600	(24%)	4,900	(14.5%)

Source: Census of India, 1931 (compiled from relevant provincial volumes).

relative position declined sharply in the nineteenth century. It was from the Uttar Pradesh Muslim salariat that the initial thrust of Muslim nationalism in India arose.[3]

The Bengali Muslim salariat was the largest in terms of absolute size as compared to Muslims of other provinces, even though its share of the total Bengali population was proportionately much smaller. Although more numerous, educated Bengali Muslims were underrepresented in government employment.

The Sind figures show how small the ethnic Sindhi Muslim salariat was—even these figures probably give a somewhat inflated picture of its size because there were considerable numbers of non-Sindhi Muslims employed in Sind.

The underprivileged ethnic salariat groups, not surprisingly, resented Punjabi domination in Pakistan and demanded fair shares for themselves. Overnight, the "Muslim identity," behind which the various Muslim salariat groups had rallied together in the Pakistan movement, was laid aside. The regional ethnic identities of the respective salariat groups were affirmed forcefully—Bengali, Sindhi, Pathan, and Baluch. Political alignments were redefined with the regional groups drawing upon their separate regional histories, languages and cultures to nourish their ethnic identities. Because the slogan of Islam was being used to beat them down, the regional salariats expressed their politics in explicitly secular terms. We find here parallels with India's past, for now the Indian slogan of "akhand Bharat" was echoed by the Punjabi slogan of the indivisibility of the Muslim nation. That was meant to imply that a person could not legitimately declare himself or herself to be Bengali or Sindhi or Pathan or Baluch, because he or she was a Muslim and Islam would recognize no divisions amongst the people of the faith. It is in that context and for that purpose that Islamic ideology was first placed at the center of political debate, only after Pakistan was created.

At first, after the creation of Pakistan, Islamic ideology was invoked only nominally, as a slogan and not much more. The bureaucratic-military oligarchy that rules Pakistan, in which the Punjabi salariat is predominant, had no intention, thereby, of allowing mullahs and Islamic ideologues to encroach on their monopoly of power and privilege.[4] Insofar as the slogan of "Islam in danger" was introduced into the vocabulary of political debate in Pakistan during the first thirty years, only a few symbolic concessions were made to men of religion to make the argument look convincing.

It was only after the seizure of power by the Zia regime that Islamic ideology was invoked in a rather more strident manner for a new purpose, namely the validation of state power for a politically bankrupt regime that lacked legitimate authority. Zia's government has had to go much farther in affirming, symbolically, its commitment to Islam than has any previous regime. But the issue of Punjabi dominance (Urdu-speaking migrants from India who had shared that position with the Punjabis gradually having fallen behind) has not thereby been displaced by the politics of Islamic ideology, for it has been recognized by oppositional groups that this is only a cover for continued Punjabi domination. Ethnicity and religious ideology therefore remain closely intertwined and the various disaffected regional groups are unimpressed by the dramaturgy of religious fervour.

ISLAMIC AND SECULAR IDEOLOGIES OF MUSLIMS IN PRE-INDEPENDENCE INDIA

There is a widespread tendency, amongst scholars as well as politicians, to attribute aspirations, political positions, and ideological orientations to Muslims of India, as if Muslim members of different social strata and in different regions all held them equally. That, of course, is manifestly untrue and, more to the point, very misleading and unhelpful if we wish to get the different movements and ideological tendencies into some perspective. Particularly interesting to note is that there was a sharp difference in such orientations between Muslim majority and Muslim minority provinces of India. It is in the latter, especially in Uttar Pradesh, that specifically Muslim political and ideological movements were generated. It may seem paradoxical to those who assume that a commitment to Muslim political identification and Islamic ideology follows from the fact of being Muslim, that in Muslim majority provinces, until the late 1940s—virtually until the eve of Partition—the rural power bases were dominated not by Islamic politics but by noncommunal groups and political parties controlling the respective governments. We can broadly identify eight ideological-political positions among Indian Muslims before Independence along with the groups holding them:

1. Islamic Traditionalism: The "Ulema I: Deobandi"
2. Islamic Traditionalism: The "Ulema II: Barelvi and Pirs"
3. Islamic Modernism: Sir Sayyid Ahmad Khan and Mohammad Iqbal
4. Islamic Fundamentalism: Maududi and Jama'at-i-Islami
6. Secular Provincial Noncommunal Transactionalism: Landlord-dominated right-wing Punjab Unionist Party and various political groups in Sind, being the ruling groups/parties
7. Secular Provincial Noncommunal Radicalism: The ruling Krishak Proja Party of Bengal, led by A. K. Fazlul Haq
8. Secular Noncommunal Nationalism: The Congress Party, being the ruling party in the Northwest Frontier Province.

In addition to the above-mentioned groups are the Shi'as, comprising about 15 percent of the population of Pakistan. While some Shi'as had organized the All-India Shi'a Conference in 1907 to rival Sunni organizations, most leading Shi'as were active in the Muslim League.[5]

Though the traditionalist Deobandi, Barelvi, and Jama'at-i-Islami all consisted of Sunni Hanafis, their ideas were quite incompatible with one another. The 'ulema of the Deobandis and Barelvis differed in many respects, by virtue of their different doctrinal positions, the different classes and regions they influenced, and their different political stances. The hallmark of the Deobandi 'ulema was their unremitting anticolonialism. Unlike the Deobandi 'ulema, however, Barelvis and pirs, as a group, were not involved in anticolonial ideology and struggle. On the contrary, most of them supported the colonial regime and were in turn favored by it.

The Deobandi 'Ulema

It took the Deobandi 'ulema many decades before they began to show their deep resentment of British rule. One should add, parenthetically, that the label Deobandi is not wholly appropriate here except for its brevity, for the eponymous Dar-ul-Uloom at Deoband was not founded until 1867. The belated hostility of these 'ulema to British rule was derived from changes brought about by the colonial state during the middle decades of the nineteenth century that directly impinged upon their lives and livelihood.

There were three contexts in which the changes affected them. Firstly, in precolonial India, Muslim 'ulema and Hindu *pandits* (priests) played a central role in the judicial system and held lucrative and influential positions. That continued during the early years of colonial rule. However, a new legal system was established to meet the needs of the expanding colonial capitalist economy. The old feudal dispensations were no longer appropriate. Along with the new laws and new types of courts to adjudicate them, a new class of English-educated lawyers and judges took over from the 'ulema, pushing them out of their influential high status and lucrative jobs.

Secondly, the 'ulema were also pushed out of the educational system. That process was a bit slower, though not because the colonial regime spared any efforts to speed it up. The regime needed Indian clerks educated to serve in the apparatus of colonial government. The traditional schools run by 'ulema and pandits, with their emphasis on classical learning, were not suited to that purpose. So they were replaced by new Anglo-vernacular schools, with the active sponsorship of the colonial state. The hostility of the 'ulema to the colonial regime no doubt owed much to these bread and butter issues, although it was legitimized and expressed in terms of moral outrage.

The third factor underlying the anticolonialism of the 'ulema was the plight of Indian weavers, the *julahas*, who were their most fervent followers. Indian weavers, once the most prosperous of the Indian artisan classes, were devastated by the colonial impact and consequent destruction of Indian textile manufacturing. Julahas were therefore among the most embittered opponents of colonialism, and developed an uncompromising attitude towards the West. The 'ulema's outlook also reflected that attitude.

These factors bound the 'ulema to the Indian nationalist cause. They never argued for the formation of an "Islamic" state or a Muslim state. Quite the contrary, they called upon Muslims to join hands with their Hindu brothers in the patriotic cause of opposing foreign rule. To rationalize that position, they put forward a theory[*] that constituted an essentially secular public philosophy. They separated the domain of faith, as a private domain, from the public domain of politics and government. This was formulated quite explicitly by Maulana Hasan Ahmad Madani of the Deoband School who argued (1) that faith was universal and could not be contained within national boundaries but (2) that nationality was a matter of geography and Muslims were bound to the nation of their birth by obligations of loyalty along with their non-Muslim fellow citizens. They would live together in harmony in independent India which, although not *dar-ul-Islam* (under Muslim rule), would be *dar-ul-amn* (the land of peace), where Muslims would be guaranteed freedom to practice their faith and where it would be their duty to live as loyal and law-abiding citizens. It was as much the duty of the Muslim in India to fight with a sense of dedication for the freedom and independence of his country as it was his duty to fight for the liberty of his conscience and the sanctity of his faith. The political philosophy of the 'ulema was a peculiar amalgam of pan-Islamic and Indian nationalist ideas which were fused in their common anti-imperialism (Faruqi 1963; Metcalf 1982). It was during the Khilafat movement (1919–23) that the Deobandi 'ulema made their biggest, though somewhat brief, impact on the Indian political scene. The aim of the movement was to restore the Ottoman Caliph to his high office, and ran counter to the aspirations of Turkish and Arab nationalists. The movement promised to isolate the Muslim salariat leadership from the Muslim masses by arousing their fanatical passions for a hopeless and anachronistic cause. The movement left behind a bitter legacy of narrow communalism, especially amongst some sections of the Muslim urban subordinate classes.

In the late 1940s, the Muslim League made great efforts to win over the 'ulema to the Pakistan cause. In November 1945, when Pakistan was already in prospect, the League findly succeeded in winning over a breakaway group, which formed the Jamiat-i-ulema-i-Islam and has since established itself as a political party within Pakistan.

Barelvi 'Ulema and Pirs

In contrast to the Deobandi 'ulema, Barelvis profess a more populist Islam, more infused with the superstition and syncretism that make up the religious beliefs of the peasantry. The name of the group derives from the name of the town of Bareilly in Uttar Pradesh, which was the seat of their mentor Maulana Ahmad Raza Khan Barelvi. The Barelvi version of Islam emphasizes belief in miracles and the powers of saints and *pirs*, worship at shrines, and the dispensing of amulets and charms, all of which are condemned by Deobandis as un-Islamic. Deobandis and Barelvis detest each other, and much sectarian conflict consists of fights between the two groups.

Pirs (Sufi *shaikhs*) play an important part in the religious life of the peasantry. Barelvi Islam is closely tied to devotion to pirs. It stresses powers of intercession of pirs. In the course of extended research in Punjabi villages, however, I found that the peasant looks up to living pirs only for specific remedies which he buys from them, rather than for eternal salvation through sustained devotion. For the latter, he worships at shrines where he communes with the spirits of dead pirs, saints who he believes can hear his prayers. He does not, therefore, regard as particularly important or worthy of reverence the *Sajjada Nashins* (guardians of the shrines), who are usually descendants of the dead saint. As for his transactional relationship with living pirs, he believes they can make barren wombs fertile, or ease the pain of incurable disease. The peasant expects to pay for any of such remedies. Where he or she is not specifically a *mureed* (disciple) of the pir, that is, when no oath of allegiance has been taken to the pir, nothing more is owed. The widely-held idea that pirs have some kind of generalized charismatic power over the peasantry whom they can move into political action at their bidding does not appear to be valid from my own case studies; where a pir does have local-level political power—and this is frequently the case—it is invariably by virtue of his being a powerful landowner in his own right and a leader or an influential member of a political faction. Recruitment of peasants by such pirs takes place on the basis of distinctly non-spiritual powers.[6]

Deobandi and Barelvi 'Ulema in Pakistan

Historically, Deobandis have tended to be mainly urban and from the middle or upper strata of society, while Barelvi influence has been mainly in rural areas, with a populist appeal. This has changed somewhat in recent decades, for Barelvi influence has extended to towns and cities amongst the lumpen-proletariat (peasants in cities) and an insecure urban petit bourgeoisie. Traditionally, Barelvi influence has been stronger in the Punjab and to some degree in Sind than in Uttar Pradesh. On the other hand, the main base of the Deobandis was in Uttar Pradesh, especially among urban Muslims. Since the creation of Pakistan, they have had some influence amongst muhajirs, the migrants from India. They are also well entrenched amongst Pathans of Sarhad (the North West Frontier province) and in the northern districts of Baluchistan, an influence that now extends to Pathan workers in Pakistan's cities, particularly Karachi.

In Pakistan, both Deobandis and Barelvis have organized themselves as political parties, the former as the Jamiat-i-ulema-i-Islam (JUI), founded in November 1945, and the latter as the Jamiat-i-ulema-i-Pakistan (JUP), which was founded in 1948. The political influence of each is much more limited than its sectarian following. In Pakistan's first general election in 1970, the Jamiat-i-ulema-i-Islam only won 7 seats out of a total of 138 for West Pakistan. Not surprisingly, 6 of these were from Sarhad and one from a Pathan constituency in Baluchistan. The JUP also won 7 seats, all from West Pakistan, of which 4 were from Punjab and 3 from Sind (1 of which was from the city of Karachi) (Ahmad 1976). In both cases, the rural seats were won not so much on the strength of religious commitment to the party concerned but rather because the JUI candidates were allied to influential tribal leaders and the JUP had relied on powerful landlords and pirs.

There is a doctrinal point which is pivotal in the political debate between these 'ulema and the Islamic fundamentalists on the one hand, and Islamic modernists on the other. That is the concept of ijtihad, the interpretative development of doctrine in keeping with the spirit of Islam on issues which cannot otherwise be clearly decided from the shari'a. The traditionalist 'ulema will not accept ijtihad. For them, the doctrine is fixed for eternity, and consists of the teachings of the four Sunni schools of law. Islamic fundamentalists and modernists reject this traditionalist view of the immutability and rigidity of the doctrine of the faith, the principle of *taqlid* (doctrinal conformity), that the 'ulema consider to be fundamental. Instead, they insist on both the possibility and the necessity of ijtihad to revivify Islam in the face of new questions and issues that arise with new conditions. The different political positions of Traditionalists, Fundamentalists, and Modernists turn on their different solutions to the question of ijtihad.

Islamic Modernism: Sir Sayyid Ahmad Khan and Mohammad Iqbal

The colonial restructuring of India's political economy shifted the base of status and influence, to some degree, away from the landed gentry and towards the emerging salariat: the members of the colonial bureaucratized state, the new aristocracy. This newly-emerging class had different needs and a different outlook from the pre-colonial upper classes. The salariat began to develop a new lifestyle and new ways. These found expression in new ideologies that took the form of religious "renaissances," first by the Hindus and then by the Muslims. Sir Sayyid Ahmad Khan was the most outstanding figure of the "Muslim renaissance," and was both an effective organizer and a major intellectual figure. His mission in life was to facilitate the transition of upper-class Uttar Pradesh Muslims into the colonial salariat. Therefore, he encouraged them to move out of the traditional system of education which was controlled by the 'ulema and instead take to English and Western education. His own life reflects such a transition from the old Uttar Pradesh aristocracy to the new salariat. He was from a noble family, with long connections to Imperial rule, which had become less prosperous. He joined the service of the East India Company against the wishes of his family, and rose to be a *munsif* (sub-judge). He soon became the leading pioneer of new liberal ideas expressed in the idiom of Islam, and was much attacked and reviled by the 'ulema. Embroidered tales of his persecution have become a part of the mythology of the Muslim salariat.

Sir Sayyid, the father of Islamic modernism, was directly influenced by Raja Ram Mohan Roy, the father of Hindu Renaissance.[7] It is no accident that parallel religious reform movements arose in different parts of India amongst both Hindus and Muslims during the mid-nineteenth century, for they all reflected similar social developments, the emergence of different sections of the same class, the new salariat. It might be more illuminating, therefore, to think of these sections as different ethnic components of a single class, and of the Hindu and Muslim reform movements as different strands of a single intellectual movement expressing the liberal ideology, rationalism, and a commitment to a scientific outlook of the newly emerging Hindu and Muslim salariats in their respective religious idioms.

As appropriate to the concerns of the emerging Muslim salariat in Uttar Pradesh, Sir Sayyid's political philosophy was cast in ethnic terms, supporting numerical equality for Muslims and Hindus in the services, even though in Uttar Pradesh Muslims comprised only about 13 percent of the population. Sir Sayyid argued that Muslims, as a community, were entitled to an equal share because they made up for their lack of overall numbers by their preponderance amongst the upper classes. That view did not entail hostility towards Hindus as such, nor was it a question of religion. The issue was that of equating the two communities, irrespective of their relative size, and demanding an equal share for each. This was nicely expressed in his much-quoted statement that India was a bride adorned by Hindus and Muslims who were her two beautiful eyes. The bride would be disfigured if the two eyes were not equal.

Sir Sayyid did not argue for a restoration of Muslim power, much less an Islamic state. Nor did he argue for independence or democracy. His hopes were pinned, rather, on an indefinite continuation of British rule, for it was the only impartial guarantee of protection of Muslim interests, which lay in Muslim's securing equality within the Indian salariat. Education was the sovereign remedy for the decline of Muslim society. The main thrust of Sir Sayyid's writing and indefatigable organizational activity, therefore, lay in the pursuit of modern education for Muslims. He was very suspicious of the Indian National Congress, and feared that independence and democracy would mean that Hindus would overwhelm the small numbers of upper-class Muslims who would then have no one to protect them. It is clear from this that his political horizons were defined by the boundaries of Uttar Pradesh, and that he did not extend the logic of his argument to Muslim majority provinces. His interpretation of liberalism was mediated by the colonial situation and his commitment to the interests of the upper classes of Uttar Pradesh. It was not, therefore, a message of freedom and independence nor of equality between individuals in society.

Mohammad Iqbal propounded a liberal Islamic political philosophy, which went a step beyond that of Sir Sayyid. Iqbal passionately attacked the 'ulema's commitment to the principle of taqlid (doctrinal conformity), which he argued had ossified Islam and made it remote from the realities of the contemporary world. Taqlid, he believed, was the root cause of the present decline of Muslims. To revitalize Muslim society, ijtihad had to be reinstated through ijma (consensus of the community) (Iqbal 1958:173). He argued further that "the transfer of ijtihad from individual representatives of schools to a legislative assembly . . . is the only possible form ijma can take in modern times" (Iqbal 1958:174).

Furthermore, referring to provisions of the Persian constitution of 1906, he repudiated as "dangerous" the idea of giving the 'ulema power to supervise legislative activity. By his idea of securing ijma through a legislative body, he legitimized the liberal principle of representative self-government, the system that the political leadership of the professionals and the salariat (though not necessarily its bureaucratic and military components) best understood and wanted.

Islamic Fundamentalism

While each of the above three groups was identified with certain social classes whose concerns and aspirations it expressed, the social roots of the Islamic fundamentalism of the Jama'at-i-Islami cannot be so clearly identified. It originated entirely as an ideological movement and its appeal was initially limited to a small number of dedicated followers to whom it offered a dream of a utopian future. It drew to itself a small band of dedicated idealists. But that has changed radically, as this account will show, for the Jama'at was soon to receive generous support from powerful vested interests for whom it began to serve a purpose.

Maulana Maududi, an opponent of Muslim nationalism and the Pakistan movement, founded the Jama'at in 1941, but considered it prudent to migrate to Pakistan after its creation. After that, his political philosophy went through a radical transformation. Maududi's opposition to the Pakistan movement had been on the grounds that the true vocation of an Islamic militant was a proselytizing one and that Islam was a universal religion that knew of no national boundaries. After the creation of Pakistan, Maududi revised the conception of his mission and that of the rationale of the Pakistan movement, arguing that its sole object had been the establishment of an Islamic state and that his party alone possessed the understanding and commitment needed to bring that about.

To build an Islamic state, the existing state must first be captured and brought under the control of those who, by Maududi's definition, were the only true bearers of militant and authentic Islam, namely himself and his party members. Unlike the 'ulema, control of the state apparatus was therefore his first priority. His conception was that an Islamic state should be strongly centralized and run on authoritarian lines, with the help of a strong, effective, and dedicated army under the control of the Commander of the Faithful. Democracy was disdained, for it gave power to the ignorant and those whose commitment to and understanding of the faith could be doubtful. The onus lay, therefore, on his party and on himself as its guide and leader to take Muslim society forward to its true destiny. The constitution of his party illustrates this authoritarian philosophy, for it demands unquestioning and total obediance from members of the party to its Amir, its supreme head, namely himself. His ideas justifying dictatorship in the name of Islam have not, surprisingly, found much favor with Pakistan's authoritarian military rulers.

The Jama'at is based on selected cadre members, and as such has not been very effective as a mass political party. The full extent of its isolation from popular support was brought home by its debacle in the controlled elections staged by the Zia regime in February 1985, as conditions for its electoral success could not have been made more favorable. All opposition parties were under a ban and their leaders and other local activists were in prison or in exile. The field was clear for the Jama'at to make a clean sweep of it, but the party was routed completely. The electorate voted negatively, against Jama'at candidates, for nonentities, some of whom are now cultivating their own credibility and building political capital on which to establish their future political careers.

Despite the Jama'at's electoral defeat, its power and influence in today's Pakistan should not be underestimated, for it is derived from the group's symbiotic relationship with the ruling regime. It tends to function as a pressure group rather than a political party and uses its influence with government agencies to achieve its objectives. The Jama'at has acquired a firm grip over the universities and wields a powerful influence over the government-owned and controlled broadcast media.

While the Jama'at, directly following Partition, enjoyed the support of the muhajirs due to their bitterness towards India as a result of their forced migration, this support has gradually withered away. Those muhajirs who settled in the interior of Sind have developed links with the local Sindhi community as traders and professionals who serve the peasants and landlords. They have, in effect, become the "New Sindhis," and tend to sympathize with the Sindhi movement which has grown quite powerful in recent years. Even in Karachi, where muhajir backing for the Sindhi movement is considerably less, outspoken leaders of the Jama'at such as Professor Ghafoor Ahmad and Jan Mohammad Abbasi have been critical of their party's support of government repression of the Sindhi movement under martial law, seeing it as diminishing the party's popular support.

Since Maududi's death in 1979, the leadership of the Jama'at has passed into nonideologist hands, although advocation of its ideology remains their principal political weapon. The leaders seem to feel that the party's diminishing base among the populace is of less consequence than the support it is deriving from powerful classes in Pakistan for whom its value lies in its ability to bludgeon radical and left-wing groups (very often quite literally). The party receives generous donations from big businessmen and landlords, and is believed by some to be a recipient of generous donations from the United States and the Middle East.

However, an excess of money and, for that matter, influence, has also brought problems for the party. New vested interests have grown up in its bureaucracy, and its old ideological wing, in decline, resents that. It appears that there is considerable tension between the ideologists in the party (mainly Karachi-based), and those whose political ambitions lie in what they can gain from their relationship with the military regime. The latter consists mainly of the Punjab-based "pragmatic" wing of the Jama'at led by Mian Tufail Mohammad, Maududi's successor. Mohammed had tendered his resignation following the Jama'at's electoral defeat. The party has now begun to voice carefully measured criticism of the government, to distance itself from it and retrieve a measure of standing among the people.

To conclude our account of the Jama'at-i-Islami, we return to the central doctrinal issue of ijtihad. The Jama'at stands for ijtihad, contrary to the traditionalist 'ulema position, but at the same time it derides the method proposed by the Modernist Iqbal for achieving it under contemporary conditions by legitimating representative democracy in the name of ijma. Maududi contended that this could not lead to a reliable interpretation of Islam, for the voters may either not be Muslims or, if they are, may not have a "true understanding" of Islam—such as that possessed by himself and his followers. Iqbal's exhortation to educate the people was no solution either Maududi argued; scholarship is no guarantee of understanding when even the Traditionalist 'ulema are misled and ignorant.

Paradoxically, Maududi's elitism itself militates against a principle regarded as a central tenet of Islam, namely that ijtihad by ijma, the consensus of the community, has precedence over ijtihad by the *alim*, the man of religious learning, because an individual, however learned, is fallible, but Allah in his mercy would not allow his community collectively to go in error. While this has been recognized as the basis of the principle of democracy in Islam, Maududi's argument contradicts it.

Secular Muslim Nationalism and Other Secular Positions

Most of the salariat, implicitly or explicitly, espoused a secular conception of being part of a Muslim nation. Jinnah, their spokesman, was always quite explicit on this issue. However, in recent years, there has been a systematic attempt by Pakistan's captive media to misrepresent Jinnah on this point, and they have tried hard to build up an image of the Father of the Nation as a religious bigot. The reality was very different. Jinnah was a member of cosmopolitan Bombay society, a close colleague and friend of Sir Pherozeshah Mehta, a Parsi Indian nationalist, and, along with M. K. Gandhi, a protégé and close friend of G. K. Gokhale, the great Indian liberal leader. Jinnah began as an active member of the Congress Party and conceived his role as a spokesman of Muslims within the Nationalist movement. He was not among the founders of the Muslim League, though he joined it later, in 1913, by invitation from League leaders. By this time, the Congress and the Muslim League were already drawing steadily closer together, holding their annual conferences at the same time and in the same place. The high point of that rapproachment was the Lucknow Pact of 1916 between the Congress and the League. Ironically, the basis of that growing unity was destroyed by a decision to pander to Muslim bigotry not by the League but by the Congress; much to the distress and resentment of the League leadership, Gandhi decided to back fanatical Muslim 'ulema in launching the Khilafat movement. If Congress had intended to drive a wedge between the secular-minded Muslim salariat and the Muslim masses, and to shift leadership in the direction of the obscurantist 'ulema, it could not have taken up a more potent issue.

Muslim notables, so-called "feudals," presided over the birth of the Muslim League in December 1906 at Dacca. Control of the League was soon taken over by representatives of the Muslim salariat, initially based at Aligarh and then at Lucknow. That is the nub of a complicated story, of which a most perceptive account is found in Robinson's (1974) excellent study of the early Muslim movement in Uttar Pradesh. Naturally, as in all great political and social movements, many different strands are interwoven in the tapestry of Muslim history in India during the nineteenth and twentieth centuries. But it is important to recognize the central part played by the salariat in Muslim nationalism in India.

A number of factors contributed to a new turn in the political development of India by the middle of the first decade of this century. The Muslim salariat was now detached from its earlier dependence on the goodwill and patronage of the colonial regime and had turned towards its own self-reliant political organization, against a background of prospective constitutional changes. In that process the Muslim salariat began to crystallize its political identity. Its key objectives were again defined by the minority position of Muslims in Uttar Pradesh rather than by their position in provinces with a Muslim majority, for its central demand was for separate electorates for Muslims so that they might not be outvoted by Hindus. Robinson (1974:173–75) sums up the results of developments in the first decade of the century as follows: "By 1909 a Muslim identity was firmly established in Indian politics . . . [by virtue of] the creation of a Muslim political organization . . . [and] the winning of separate Muslim electorates. . . . The creation of a protected share of power for Muslims . . . stimulated the further development of Muslim politics."

Jinnah reassessed the situation and recognized a role for himself as a spokesman for Muslims in the Nationalist movement on the strength of their independent organization in the Muslim League. Robinson

(1974:252) comments: "He brought to the League leadership important connections with all-Indian Congress circles and the distinction of having been a close friend of Gokhale."

Jinnah was increasingly disenchanted with the leadership of the Indian National Congress. The failure to reach an accomodation with the Congress after the 1937 elections finally forced him to reconsider his strategy. Up to that point the Muslim League's influence had been limited to the salariat: thus its poor showing in elections in a nation where landlords controlled the dominant rural vote. After the 1937 elections, Jinnah decided to secure Muslim landlord support at any price and set about making deals with those in power in Muslim majority provinces, persuading them to accept the Muslim League label even if only nominally. In return, he gave them carte blanche, in effect surrendering the local Muslim League organizations to them. His objective was to make the Muslim League, at least nominally, the "ruling party" in Muslim majority provinces. That would legitimize his claim that the Muslim League was the sole and legitimate voice of the Muslims of India.

Jinnah looked upon the landed magnates, the political bosses of the Muslim majority provinces, with dislike and contempt. They in turn showed little inclination to allow him and the central Muslim League leadership to encroach on their domains of power. In Punjab, where the political division was urban-rural, the rural magnates heading the Unionist Party had opposed the urban salariat, which was the Muslim League's mainstay. The Unionist Party, under Sir Fazl-i-Husain, was determined to keep Punjab politics "non communal." Fazl-i-Husain's closest and most trusted associate was Sir Chhotu Ram, a Hindu. Iqbal complained of Sir Fazl-i-Husain's anti-urban bias in a speech in 1935, as did his associate Malik Barkat Ali; both were urban stalwarts of the Muslim League (Husain 1946:315–16). Later, Iqbal was to repeatedly criticize Jinnah's 1936 pact with Sir Sikandar Hayat, Sir Fazl-i-Husain's successor. This was the first of many one-sided arrangements between the Unionist Party and the Muslim League: in return for the Unionists' nominal allegiance to the Muslim League, it delivered the Punjab branch of the League into Sir Sikander Hayat's hands. In a series of letters in October and November 1937, Iqbal complained to Jinnah that "Sir Sikandar wants nothing less than complete control of the League and the Provincial Parliamentary Board" (Iqbal 1963:28–32). Jinnah maintained a prudent silence over the matter and did not reply to Iqbal's repeated letters; having handed over the Punjab branch to the Unionists, there was little that he could have said.

In Sind, the story was no different, for there the local base of the

Muslim salariat was narrower than that in the Punjab. The urban leadership of the Muslim League, mainly in Karachi, was largely ethnic non-Sindhi. The rural ethnic Sindhi leadership was divided into warring factions led by Ghulam Hussain Hidayatullah and G. M. Syed. The social composition of Hidayatullah's faction was a replica of that of the Punjab Unionist Party. Jinnah decided to put his bet on the more powerful Hidayatullah faction, but it was evidently an unpalatable decision. Jinnah confided his views about his party colleagues to Sir Hugh Dow, Governor of Sind (which itself is an extraordinary reflection on Jinnah's relationship with the servitors of Empire). Dow, in a Secret letter reporting on political developments to Wavell, the Viceroy, wrote: "Jinnah made a prolonged stay in Karachi . . . and held prolonged conferences with the 'leaders' . . . Jinnah dislikes them all (he once told me that he could buy the lot of them for 5 lakhs of rupees to which I replied that I could do it much cheaper) and has been mainly concerned that the League ticket should go to the man who was most likely to be returned, his previous and subsequent loyalty to the League being a minor consideration."[8] All that Jinnah wanted was to pin the Muslim League label on the provincial government.

It is not difficult to see the short-term benefits of this strategy for Jinnah, for it legitimized his all-India stance and strengthened his bargaining position. The reason the provincial magnates accepted the Muslim League label is less obvious. It was not for the League's vote-pulling power, for it was the landed magnates themselves who controlled the mainly rural vote. What the League offered is clear only if we consider the fundamental shift in the long-term political picture in India as independence approached. This was finally becoming visible to the landed magnates, whose eyes had previously focused too narrowly on the provincial scene. With independence in sight, they had to look beyond their provincial horizons; some of them could see the writing on the wall earlier than others. It was clear that it was only a matter of time before colonial rule ended. With the departure of their colonial patrons, the landed magnates were faced with the prospect of rule by the Congress Party, with its commitment to land reform. If they were to preserve their class position, their only viable option was rule by the Muslim League. If that meant the formation of Pakistan—whatever its nature—it would in any case guarantee their own survival, for the Muslim League was wholly dependent on them. They would wield power in any autonomous regional grouping of Muslim majority provinces that would ensue. In effect, Pakistan would guarantee their class survival. It was not ideology but clearly understood self-interest that lined them up behind the Muslim League. They were unimpressed by Muslim League politics until independence was imminent. Only then did they decide to jump onto the Muslim League bandwagon and, in fact, take it over.

When the Pakistan slogan was coined, Jinnah's opponents continually complained that he was refusing to specify precisely what Pakistan was actually to be. Evidently, as a seasoned negotiator, Jinnah did not lay all his cards prematurely on the table. But it was not difficult to see that he was aiming for a grouping of Muslim majority provinces enjoying a degree of regional autonomy, possibly within an overall Indian federal union, rather than the partition of India, especially if that entailed carving up Punjab and Bengal. That he was quite happy to accept Pakistan as a regional grouping within an Indian federal union is supported by his ready acceptance of the three-tier Cabinet Mission Plan, which offered just that in April 1946. It was the Congress Party which rejected it. The logic of the federal union solution was particularly important for Muslims in Muslim minority provinces, for it would establish a link between them and those in power in Muslim majority regions within the federal union. That would be a guarantee for reciprocal protection of the interests of both Muslim and Hindu minorities in the respective regions, or so it was thought.

The carving up of Punjab and Bengal that accompanied the Partition of India was the result of the ironical turn taken by Indian politics in that fateful month of May 1946 when Congress forced the issue. This was already decided by them on 2 June, when Mountbatten gave Jinnah a bare fourteen hours to consider the future and the fate of his people, for he was given the Mountbatten Plan at 10 A.M., a definite reply being demanded by midnight. Jinnah pleaded for time—a week—but was refused. The insensitive and unsympathetic account given by Campbell-Johnson (1951:102–103), a Mountbatten aide, is nevertheless quite poignant, for Jinnah, feeling defeated at the final moment, was literally speechless and could bring himself to do no more than nod to indicate his agreement of the June 3rd Plan. This was no moment of glory.

Jinnah had consistently opposed theocratic ideas and influences, and never minced his words about his commitment to a secular state. Speaking to students of Aligarh Muslim University, the heart of the Muslim salariat, in February 1938, he declared: "What the League has done is to set you free from the reactionary elements of Muslims and to create the opinion that those who play their selfish game are traitors. It has certainly freed you from that undesirable element of Maulvis and Maulanas." [a derogatory reference to the 'ulema] (Ahmad, 1952:43) He reiterated, time and again, that Pakistan would be "without any distinction of caste, creed or sect." His inaugural address to the Pakistan Constituent Assembly on 11 August 1947 was a clarion call for the establishment of Pakistan as a secular state. From the principal forum of the new state he declared: "You may belong to any religion or caste or creed—that has nothing to do with the business of the state . . . We are starting with this fundamental principle, that we are all citizens of one state" (Choudhury, 1967:21–22). There could be no clearer statement of the secular principle as the basis of Pakistan.

A confirmation of the fact that Jinnah never made any concessions whatever to ideas about a theocratic state comes from a somewhat unexpected source. Sharif al-Mujahid, head of the Quaid-e-azam Academy and an ideologue of the Zia regime, is hard put to find even some stray remark in Jinnah's vast collection of speeches and writings to sustain the false image of the Father of the Nation that the Zia regime wishes to present, as an advocate of Islamic ideology and an Islamic state. In desperation, al-Mujahid (1981:230–231) concludes that: "Jinnah was a political leader and not a systematic thinker . . . For a brilliant and accomplished lawyer such as Jinnah was, his academic grounding was rather inadequate . . . Jinnah could not work out a consistent theoretical framework of Pakistan. For one thing his was not the role of a systematic theoretician nor was he qualified for it." One need not say more after this ridiculous statement and unintended testimony.

Today's true heirs of Pakistan's founding ideology are the Secularists, many of them believing Muslims, who reject and repudiate the idea of exploitation of Islamic ideology in pursuit of political ends. If Islamic Modernism was the initial ideology of the emerging Muslim salariat, it has long ceased to be a live intellectual movement and has been marginalized. It exists in small and peripheral groupings such as the Tulu-e-Islam group led by Ghulam Ahmad Parvaiz. Many of the basic ideas of Islamic Modernism have passed into conventional wisdom. Insofar as they still have currency, they are accomodated within secular political attitudes. It may help to put things into perspective to quote from an account by E. I. J. Rosenthal, a renowned Islamic scholar, of his investigations in Pakistan, even though his report is two decades old. He summed up his impressions of attitudes in Pakistan thus: "On balance, I should say that among the academic youth there is a minority in favor of an Islamic state in substance, not just in name. The majority are divided in their allegiance to Islam from personal faith to indifference and outright rejection as being out of date and dividing men instead of unifying and leading them to a world state" (Rosenthal 1965:245). More recently, this issue has been dealt with sensitively and perceptively by Sibte Hassan (1983) in his influential book *Naveed-e-Fikr*, where he arrives at similar conclusions.

ISLAM, ETHNICITY AND THE POST-INDEPENDENT PERIOD

Muslim ethnicity had outlived its original purpose when Pakistan was created, for the Muslim salariat no longer stood in opposition to Hindus. Instead, a new dominant ethnic group identified itself, the ruling Punjabis. In turn, other sections of the once Muslim salariat now redefined their ethnic identities, seeing themselves as Bengalis, Sindhis, Pathans, or Baluchis who were underprivileged in the new state and wanted fairer shares for themselves. These groups had left Muslim ethnicity behind in the pre-Partition world. Now the issue of regional balance was to be at the center of politics in Pakistan, ill-concealed by the rhetoric of Islamic ideology that was deployed against regional groups, denying the legitimacy of their newly affirmed separate identities.

A fresh process of accounting was devised to accent regional privilege and deprivation. Although there were 41.9 million East Pakistanis, as against only 33.7 million West Pakistanis (1951 census), shares in public appointments did not reflect that ratio even remotely. In 1948, East Pakistanis held only 11 percent of jobs in Pakistan's civil service, the elite core controlling the bureaucracy and thereby the state in Pakistan. The East Pakistani share in the army was even smaller; only 1.5 percent of army officers were East Pakistanis. Their share in private business was also disproportionate; Bengali Muslims owned no more than 3.5 percent of the assets of all private Muslim firms (Jahan 1972:25–27).

As this imbalance became clear, a wave of political militancy swept through the whole of East Pakistan. The Bengali Language Movement erupted with dramatic force in February 1952 when, for a few days, the writ of the Government ceased to run in the province. Every Bengali government employee went on strike. That movement, significantly, started on the Dacca University campus. The movement repudiated the ruling Muslim League's claim to represent the people of East Pakistan. In the 1954 provincial elections, the ruling Muslim League party won no more than 10 seats out of a total of 309, notwithstanding its repression of opposition parties and the fact that many of the elected candidates were in prison at the time. The opposition United Front party, which articulated Bengali nationalism, swept the elections. Sindhi, Pathan, and Baluch movements were soon to develop likewise in West Pakistan.

At first, the secular tradition of Jinnah was maintained in Pakistan. In March 1949, moving the "Objectives Resolution" in the Constituent Assembly, Prime Minister Liaquat Ali Khan declared: "The people are the real recipients of power. This naturally eliminates any danger of the establishment of a theocracy" (Choudhury 1967:25). G. W. Choudhury, editor of *Constitutional Documents of Pakistan* and a champion of Islamic ideology, complained that "the 'ulema were also not happy with the first draft constitution as it contained very little, if at all, any (sic) provisions as to the Islamic character of the proposed constitution" (Choudhury 1967:30).

As soon as regional protests against Punjabi rule began to develop in various areas of Pakistan, however, the ideological tune changed. Suddenly Islam and the notion of Islamic brotherhood became the order of the day. It was unpatriotic on the part of Bengalis, Sindhis, Pathans, and Baluchis to make demands in terms of their regional ethnic identities because all Pakistanis were brothers in Islam. The constitutional proposals were quickly redrafted. As Choudhury happily reported: "The Second Draft Constitution (1962) was noted for elaborate provisions relating to the Islamic character of the proposed Constitution. The most noble feature of the Islamic provision was a board of 'ulema which would examine if any law was repugnant to [the] Qur'an and Sunnah" (Choudhury 1967:31).

All that this "noble feature" added up to was a smokescreen, however, for it did little beyond setting up a Board of Islamic Education which had some advisory functions. In any case, both the Constitutent Assembly and the Board of Islamic Education existed only on paper and did not really function; from the outset, the real power was held by the bureaucratic-military oligarchy, with the Punjabi salariat holding a dominant position within it.[9] The only concrete results of all this, after years of rhetorical Islamization, were a decision to change the name of the republic to "The Islamic Republic of Pakistan" and a constitutional provision that the president must be a Muslim. The ruling oligarchy made no concessions of substance to the Islamic ideologists.

The secular mood of Pakistan and ethnic divisions within it were dramatically demonstrated in the first national election in 1970. The secular Awami League, predominantly Bengali with no influence in West Pakistan, swept the board in East Pakistan, winning every seat but one; that one seat for the Chittagong Hill Tracts was uncontested to allow its tribal leader to be elected there. In West Pakistan, the Pakistan People's Party, with its secular slogan of *roti, kapra aur makan* (food, clothes, and shelter), won a landslide victory in Sind and Punjab, with the left-wing National Awami Party making a very good showing in Sarhad and Baluchistan. The Islamic parties won nowhere.

The Bengali movement was eventually to lead to the liberation of Bangladesh. It was the Bengali salariat which spearheaded the movement, although it had deep roots in the countryside. In a predominantly rural province (the urban population in 1960 being only about 5 percent), most members of the Bengali salariat were sons of well-to-do peasants or landed gentry, and got solid support from their rural power base.

A similar occurrence appears to be happening with the powerful Sindhi movement that has erupted in the last few years. Its ideology too is explicitly secular, and as in Bengal, the Sindhi salariat is backed fully by the rural population, for its members also are sons of peasants or landlords, big and small.

With the assumption of power by the Zia regime another factor has come into play, namely the legitimacy of power. Afraid to face a free electorate and having no mandate to govern, Zia has turned to Allah. He has been forced to go far beyond the worn out old rhetoric and show to a cynical public that he actually means business. There is not much that he can do in practice, at least with regard to the economy; he must run a peripheral capitalist economy which has its own rules, logic, and imperatives that he cannot afford to disregard or interfere with. So he has drawn the line clearly. He will make symbolic changes instead. In the act setting up Shariat Courts,[10] everything connected with the working of the economy is explicitly excluded from their jurisdiction, under subsection (c) of section 203 A.

All that is left for the regime to do, in the name of Islamization, is to undertake cosmetic measures, although the word "cosmetic" is an outrageous way to describe the barbaric punishments that are imposed under the hudud ordinances. The regime has also launched a systematic attack, both symbolically and practically, on the status and privileges of women in Pakistani society. That in turn has sparked off a women's movement generating a force unknown in Pakistan's history. The only measure that can properly be called cosmetic is "interest free banking," the regime's pride and joy in its record of achievements. Banks, instead of charging interest to customers, now must "buy" their customers' goods which otherwise would have been hypothecated to the bank against the loan. The bank simultaneously "resells" the same goods to the customers, at a higher price. The difference between the buying and selling prices is the "profit" that the bank earns, being in effect what used to be called interest. This is just petty deception, leaving the essentials unchanged, turning "interest" into "profit."

The Zia regime's strident rhetoric about the Islamic basis of Pakistan's ideology has failed to give it the basis of legitimacy that it has sought. On the contrary, its rhetoric has compounded its problems by raising the hopes of some naive ideologists and Islamic fundamentalists that it is in no position to fulfill. Its bigoted supporters are already becoming disillusioned and, in the light of their electoral debacle, have begun to voice criticism of the regime that has so far protected and patronized them. There are already signs that the regime has begun to soft-pedal the slogan of Islamic ideology and is trying to find alternative ways to build legitimacy. So far it has had little success.

NOTES

1. This argument, as discussed in this chapter, is an abbreviated version of a paper presented to the Middle East Discussion Group at the University of Oxford in October 1985.

2. For an example of this misconception, see Edward Mortimer, *Faith and Power: The Politics of Islam* (New York: Random House, 1982).

3. This is well documented in Francis Robinson, *Separatism among Indian Muslims: The Politics of the U.P. Muslims 1860–1923* (Cambridge University Press, 1974).

4. For an analysis of the role of the bureaucratic-military oligarchy in the state of Pakistan, see Hamza Alavi, "Class and State in Pakistan," in *Pakistan: The Roots of Dictatorship: The Political Economic of a Praetorian State*, (ed. H. N. Gardezi and J. Rashid (London: Zed Press, 1983). Within the bureaucratic-military oligarchy, the military emerged as the senior partner by the 1970s and the coherence of the once tightly knit bureaucracy, controlled by the CSP cadres, has by now been largely broken up. The Punjabi salariat dominates both the military and civil bureaucracies.

5. Some Shi'a organizations have recently surfaced in Pakistan, influenced by the government's Islamization program and the Iranian revolution. They want to be able to adhere to fiqh Jafaria, their own legal code, as opposed to the Hanafi fiqh, which is the basis of the government's program. There have been some demands by Sunnis that Hanafi fiqh be made the law of the land, and that all other sects be declared minorities and be given second class citizenship. This development is the logical extension of the claim made by the Zia regime to impose Islamic law in Pakistan; the question is, Which Islamic Law?

6. For an account of modes of operation at the village level of political factions dominated by landlords and Pirs, see Hamza Alavi, "Politics of Dependence: A village in West Punjab," *South Asian Review* 4, No. 4 (January 1971).

7. Christian W. Troll, *Sayyid Ahmad Khan: A Reinterpretation of Muslim Theology* (Karachi, 1979), 18 and note 75.

8. Dow to Wavell, 20 September 1945, *Fortnightly Reports—Sind*, L/P and J/5—261, India Office Records.

9. See note 4 above.

10. This act is found in the Constitution (Amendment) Order, 1980, issued by presidential decree.

REFERENCES

Ahmad, Iftikhar. 1976. *Pakistan General Elections 1970*. Lahore.

Ahmad, Jamil-ud-Din, ed. 1952. *Speeches and Writings of Mr. Jinnah*, Vol. 1. 6th ed.

Lahore: Mohammad Ashraf.

Aziz, K. K. 1976. *Party Politics in Pakistan, 1947–58*. Islamabad: The National Commission on Historical and Cultural Research.

Basu, Aparna. 1974. *The Growth of Education and Political Development in India 1878–1920*. Delhi.

Campbell-Johnson, A. 1951. *Mission with Mountbatten*. London: Robert Hale.

Choudhury, G. W., ed. 1967. *Documents and Speeches on the Constitution of Pakistan*. Dacca: Green Book House.

Faruqi, Zia-ul-Hassan. 1963. *The Deoband School and the Demand for Pakistan*. Bombay: Asia Publishing House.

Gardezi, H. N. and J. Rashid, eds. 1983. *Pakistan: The Roots of Dictatorship: The Political Economy of a Praetorian State*. London: Zed Press.

Hassan, S. Sibte. 1983. *Naveed-e-Fikr.* Karachi.

Husain, Azim. 1946. *Fazl-i-Husain: A Political Biography*. Bombay.

Iqbal, Mohammad. 1963. *Letters of Iqbal to Jinnah* Reprint. Lahore: Ashraf.

———. 1968. *The Reconstruction of Religious Thought in Islam*. Lahore: Ashraf.

Jahan, Rounaq. 1972. *Pakistan: Failure in National Integration*. New York: Columbia University Press.

Mansergh, N. and P. Moon, eds. 1981. *Constitutional Relations Between Britain and India: The Transfer of Power 1942–47*, Vol. 10. Document No. 229. London.

McCully, B. T. 1940. *English Education and the Origins of Indian Nationalism*. New York: Columbia University Press.

Metcalf, Barbara D. 1982. *Islamic Revival in British India: Deoband, 1860–1900*. Princeton: Princeton University Press.

al-Mujahid, Sharif. 1981. *Quaid-e-Azam Jinnah*. Karachi.

Robinson, Francis. 1974. *Separatism Among Indian Muslims: The Politics of the UP Muslims 1860–1923*. Cambridge: Cambridge University Press.

Rosenthal, E. I. J. 1965. *Islam and the Modern National State*. Cambridge: Cambridge University Press.

3

Economic Management within an Islamic Context

Shahid Javed Burki

What is meant by economic management within an Islamic context? It is important to raise the question for the simple reason that a number of countries—Pakistan, the Sudan, and Malaysia among them—have begun to experiment with new, supposedly Islamic mechanisms for raising, managing, and distributing resources. A number of other countries—Saudi Arabia, Kuwait, Libya, and Iran among them—claim that they are already operating the Islamic system. There is no doubt that still more countries from the Islamic world will seek to adopt the system—or at any rate some part of it—when those that are already experimenting with it have gained more experience.

While the question is no doubt an important one, it is not easy to answer. A well articulated explanation of what Islamic economic management is is yet to be given. Not a great deal of scholarly work has been done in this area; in the little that is available it is difficult to find agreement among scholars on a number of important issues. One way of approaching the subject is to adopt the case study method, to analyse how one country has interpreted the idea of an Islamic economic system and how it is attempting to change the old system to make it conform to this interpretation. Pakistan is the country chosen for this purpose.

The analysis that follows this brief introduction has three parts. The first provides, in outline, an assessment of the current government thinking in Pakistan of the main features of an Islamic system. There are, of course, people and institutions outside the government who are engaged in providing interpretations of what is meant by an Islamic economic system[1] and no doubt this thinking has influenced the way the government itself has interpreted the meaning of the system and the way it is implementing it. But this thinking, and the literature on which it is based, remains unfocused and discordant and is not, therefore, very helpful in understanding the practical aspects of the system. Nevertheless, an effort is made to use it here to supplement the material available from the government. The second part of this chapter identifies the various features of Pakistan's current economic situation which have the potential of being addressed by the application of Islamic thinking. The third and final part of this chapter analyzes whether the approach embodied in the Sixth Five-Year Plan (1983–88)[2] conforms to the Islamic economic system as currently defined in Pakistan. A brief concluding section will draw the lessons that may be learned from Pakistan's experience.

THE ISLAMIC ECONOMIC SYSTEM: ITS MAIN FEATURES

Perhaps the most important comprehensive statement issued by the Government of Pakistan on what it believes to be the main features of an Islamic system is contained in the *Report of the Committee on Islamization* that was commissioned in April 1980. At that time the Minister of Finance appointed a committee "to spell out an 'agenda for Islamic reform.' "[3]

The report is an interesting document for a number of reasons. To begin with, the authors of the report opted for a very gradual and deliberate process of introducing the Islamic system in Pakistan. It could not be done suddenly "since Pakistan's economy had evolved essentially on capitalist lines and, therefore, had many features that were not Islamic. True the institutions will change under the impact of Islamic Reform, but that takes time. A beginning has to be made and at this stage the institutional constraints are overwhelming. The point of contact of the Islamization process will be the present socio-economic set-up, which, being a hard reality cannot be ignored."[4]

After arguing for the need for a deliberately articulated process of Islamization, the report took the even more radical step of rejecting the notion that the establishment of an interest-free economy and the introduction of zakat were the necessary conditions for introducing an Islamic economic order. There was, in the authors' belief, "an undue obsession with only these two elements of the Islamic reform."[5] To abolish interest might produce decidedly un-Islamic results: a "rise in the overall level of economic exploitation of the poor by the rich."[6]

In the committee's view, the premature introduction of an interest-free economy could cause a serious deterioration in the distribution of income. It believed that means must not be confused with ends: the main purpose of the Islamic system of economic management was the achievement of *al-adl wal-ahsan* (justice and kindness). To bring this about, the society could select any number of means, avoiding those that would only exacerbate the situation. In the case of Pakistan, the approch needed encompassed the provision of universal education, the improvement of the quality of life through the availability and easy accesibility of basic consumer goods, and an increase in the level of employment. Obviously sensitive to potential criticism that the report proposed nothing novel or readily identifiable as purely Islamic, the committee acknowledged that "these are the objectives of any economic system; but that does not disqualify them from being the objectives of the Islamic economic system as well, particularly as they follow directly from Islam's own distinctive economic philosophy."[7]

In advocating economic growth with improved income distribution, the report made two concrete suggestions: land redistribution in which ceilings on holdings would be applied to families rather than individuals and the introduction of an inheritance tax equal to 30 percent of the deceased's wealth.[8] The first recommendation was based on an implicit recognition of the small gain accruing from previous attempts at land reform;[9] the latter was meant to prevent "intergenerational snowballing of wealth."[10]

The committee also found that in Islam the state had a significant role to play in economic management. It rejected the economic philosophy embodied in the Second Five-Year Plan (1960–65), under which the government consciously let profits multiply while increases in wages were restricted in order to maximize the flow of investible surplus in the corporate sector. "Such a strategy was based on an explicit acceptance of income and wealth differentials, which were allowed to grow even further as a means of achieving rapid growth rates."[11] The committee rejected this approach; in the Islamic system, social betterment was not to be achieved through personal greed:[12] the path to ultimate equality must not lie through initial inequality.[13] Islam, according to the committee, "would not—as it cannot—use widening income differentials as a policy instrument to promote capital formation and economic growth by virtue of its commitment to al-adl wal-ahsan.[14] It was the responsibility of the state to prevent the occurrence of a situation in which the initial cost of promoting growth was borne by the underprivileged segments of society. To prevent the poor from paying such a price:

> the public sector will be called upon in an Islamic economy to assume, among other things, a predominant role as producer of "wage goods." For social welfare requires not only a transfer of financial resources from the rich to the poor, but a diversion of real resources to the production of basic necessities of life. . . . In other words, the very composition of the "consumer goods basket" in an Islamic economy will require the state to play a tangible role in it. The matter is too important to be left to the "invisible hand" of the market forces.[15]

Once again the committee was being extraordinarily eclectic in formulating its views about the essential elements in an Islamic economic system. In suggesting that the state should play a role in fulfilling the basic needs of the poor, it was adopting a line different from that used by the regime of Zulfikar Ali Bhutto to expand the presence of the government in economic management. The nationalization of major industries, banks, and insurance companies in the early seventies was undertaken in order to get the state to occupy the "commanding heights" of the economy.[16] That move was not distributive but strategic in the sense that its aim was to reduce the considerable political and economic powers of the industrialists. The state, by assuming the control of these industries and also of the financial institutions, could channel private savings into sectors of its own choosing. However, the way this was actually done was not by emphasizing the production of the "consumer goods basket" but by building the capital goods industry. The consequence of this approach was a considerable slowdown in growth, a sharp increase in inflation, and, consequently, a deterioration in income distribution. It was the committee's new definition that would result in the improvement of the economic circumstances of the society's less priviledged groups.

Finally, the report urged upon the government an economic program that would produce a moderate rate of growth: it rejected the generation of very high rates of savings to produce rapid growth since it was un-Islamic to sacrifice the consumption levels of present generations to improve those of future generations. Once again this was a departure from the approach adopted in the past, in particular during the sixties when achieving rapid growth was regarded as the most important objective of government policy. The committee also argued against excessive foreign borrowing to promote development since that would have an impact on the levels of consumption of future generations. This was yet another departure since Pakistan had in the past relied excessively on the influx of foreign capital for domestic investment.

In sum, the report, in defining the main features of an Islamic economic system, did suggest a fairly radical departure from the way the economy was being managed. It was less radical on the question of timing: the period of transition had to be long and deliberate in order to minimize disruption. It advocated the pursuit of a moderate rate of economic growth; some redistribution of physical assets, in particular of land; a considerable improvement in the provision of social services, in particular of education; and the alleviation of poverty through a state program to give the poor access to basic goods.

Quite a profound change would have occurred in the structure and growth pattern of Pakistan's economy had the government accepted the committee's recommendations in their entirety. To begin with, the alleviation of poverty and distribution of income would have become the principal objectives of development. Consequently, the economy would have grown at a much slower rate. The dependence on injections of foreign capital would have been reduced as the generation of domestic resources was given a more important role. The state would have given up its role as a producer of capital goods and as a monopolist in the trade of some commodities. Instead, it would have concentrated its attention on producing—or helping to produce—and distributing goods needed for everyday consumption.

The government's approach towards the committee report, however, was to accept only some of its recommendations. For instance, it agreed that radical departures could not be made and that a great deal of caution should be exercised in introducing new concepts. That notwithstanding, the government went on to introduce some concepts that are identified as purely Islamic, even though the committee had clearly said that their adoption was not crucial to the introduction of an Islamic system. These include zakat (a tax on wealth); 'ushr (a tax on the produce of agricultural land); and, initially, a scheme of profit sharing adopted by the banking sector to run parallel to interest-bearing accounts. In the middle of 1984, the government announced its intention of allowing only interest-free banking from 1 January 1985. Its introduction of these measures may have been political since their public identification with the Islamic system—in particular that of zakat and interest-free banking—was strong. But at the same time it has become clear that the regime has not been prepared to rush into the Islamization of the economy. Thus in a radio and television address to the nation on 3 June 1980, President Zia ul-Haq explained why he needed more time to usher in an interest-free economy.

> The most important and difficult issue in the context of Islamic laws relates to the fiscal sector where we are trying to get rid of the curse

> of interest. You will recall that while announcing the enforcement of certain Islamic laws [last year], I had stated that we will need three years to evolve an interest-free economic system. . . . To complete the rest of the work as speedily as possible, the Committee of the financial experts functioning under the Council of Islamic Ideology is working hard with great devotion. I hope that this Committee will finalize its recommendation at the earliest.[17]

THE MAIN FEATURES OF THE PRESENT ECONOMIC SITUATION

It would be useful at this stage to summarize the main features of the present economic situation in Pakistan with a view to analyzing whether the Islamic system as defined above has any relevance. In this connection, the following five features are worth noting:

Firstly, Pakistan may soon cross over from being a poor country to being a middle income one.[18] The World Bank uses a dividing line of $410 per capita to distinguish poor from middle income countries. Pakistan's income per head for 1982 was estimtaed at $380. At the rate of growth Pakistan has experienced in the past seven years, it could cross the threshold by the end of this decade.[19]

Secondly, this extraordinary economic development has been made possible by a pronounced reliance on foreign capital. At present, Pakistan invests about 17 percent of its gross domestic product but saves only 5 percent of it, leaving a resource gap of about 12 percent.[20] This gap has been financed in part from the remittances received from Pakistani workers in the Middle East; in part from the World Bank, United States, and other donors; and in part from external borrowings. This reliance on external borrowings means that Pakistan now carries a fairly large burden of outstanding debt—estimated at about $9 billion (the equivalent of about one-third of Pakistan's gross income and about twice its total export earnings).

Thirdly, although the country has potentially one of the richest agricultural sectors anywhere in the world, land productivity remains low. It is only very recently that Pakistan has ceased to import large quantities of food grain. In 1979, for instance, more than two million tons of food grains had to be imported to give the population the minimum amount of food energy needed.

Fourthly, although the average annual growth rate of Pakistan's Gross Domestic Product over the last four decades—from Independence in 1947 to the present—has been one of the highest in the world, the level of social development remains extraordinarily low. Pakistan's infant mortality rate of 121 per thousand, child mortality rate of 17 per thousand, adult literacy rate of only 24 percent, and primary school enrollment rate of only 31 percent for females are all considerably lower than those of India even though Pakistan's income per head is 46 percent higher.[21] Other indices of social development could be cited and other comparisons made but the conclusion would be the same: Pakistan is socially much more backward than other countries at its level of per capita income.

Fifthly, Pakistan's population continues to grow very rapidly—at slightly less than 3.0 percent per annum. Without a major effort in this area, the country's population would stabilize at 377 million in the year 2035 at which point, having in the meantime overtaken the United States, Soviet Russia, Japan, Brazil, and Indonesia, it would be the fifth most populous nation in the world.[22]

In what way could the Islamic system as defined earlier influence the five features just identified? The definition of the system Pakistan is following puts great emphasis on social justice. If this were translated into practice, it could have a decisive impact on social development. The system also emphasizes a more equitable distribution of assets—in particular that of agricultural land. There is now a considerable amount of empirical evidence to suggest a positive relationship between the degree of equality in landholdings and the growth of agricultural output. Once again, a move towards Islamization should help to realize Pakistan's extraordinary agricultural potential. These are two positive features of the system. But application of the Islamic system could pose problems as well. This system does not emphasize the importance of savings; in fact, it seeks a balance between current savings and future consumption. Given the already low level of domestic savings, putting the Islamic system into practice would mean even greater reliance on foreign capital. If this were to happen, Pakistan could have serious debt and balance of payments problems before very long.[23] Secondly, the Islamic system as articulated in Pakistan makes no effort to address the problem posed by its high birth rate. In fact, in some quarters, the practice of family planning is viewed as distinctly un-Islamic. Consequently, if the birth rate remains high, the objective of social development may not be easy to achieve. A high birth rate and consequent increase in population would also mean a lower rate of growth in Gross Domestic Product per capita.

The conclusion that can be drawn from this analysis is that if the society's objectives are to be defined in conventional economic terms—that is, rapid but sustainable economic growth achieved with the maximum possible reliance on domestic resources and with the ultimate object of improving conditions for the entire population—then the Islamic system that Pakistan seems to be adopting can achieve only some of them. Such an Islamic system should improve the level of social development and further alleviate poverty; it should also bring about a significant improvement in agricultural output. But such a system would not maximize the growth of total output or reduce the dependence of the economy on foreign capital.

ISLAMIZATION AND THE SIXTH PLAN

Finally, the question must be asked, Does the Sixth Five-Year Plan—the most important economic statement issued to date by the present government—qualify as Islamic? Put this way, the question sounds rhetorical, but it is much more than that since an answer to it would indicate what progress Pakistan has made in defining a viable and workable Islamic system of economic management.

The question is not easy to answer. What is an Islamic development plan? Should it be Islamic in its objectives; Islamic in the instruments it chooses to achieve those objectives; Islamic in adopting the style of fiscal management and redistributive mechanisms that are traditionally associated with Islam? Posed this way, the question is somewhat easier to answer.

Of the seven principal objectives of the Sixth Five-Year Plan, five are fairly conventional and appeared in most of Pakistan's previous plans. They are: a high rate of growth in Gross Domestic Product; a dramatic increase in domestic savings; the development of agriculture as the lead sector of the economy; an improvement in the distribution of income; and a significant reduction in the birth rate. The sixth and seventh objectives—a dramatic improvement in the level of social development and a reduced state role in the production sectors of the economy—are new to Pakistan's development plans. As will be recalled from the discussion of the *Report of the Committee on Islamization*, these two objectives, more than any others, were identified as providing an Islamic content to an economic system. It could be said, therefore, that the Sixth Plan has introduced a decidedly Islamic slant to the process of development. But basically its approach is eclectic since it continues to emphasize the objectives that a pure Islamic plan would not have.

The choice of instruments for achieving the objectives is equally eclectic. Land reform, as may be recalled, was one of the main instruments of improving agricultural output advocated by the Committee on Islamization. However, neither land reform nor any other land distribution method has been implemented. Instead, if an instrument were to be identified as the one the plan puts most emphasis on for agricultural transformation, it is the mechanization of agriculture. But the plan does have a place for traditional Islamic instruments. Zakat is to be used for helping the destitute and for creating a safety net to catch those that a modern economic system fails to reach. 'Ushr is to be counted on for tapping the sector of agriculture for increasing domestic savings. Mosque schools are to be used for increasing the rate of enrollment for both boys and girls.

The Sixth Plan, therefore, confirms the basic approach the government appears to have adopted in moving towards Islamization. The approach is not to rush into an area that remains uncharted but to move in with a great deal of caution; not to be glib with the use of labels such as Islamic and un-Islamic; and not to define in very broad terms the meaning of an Islamic economic society.

CONCLUSION

In defining the contours of an Islamic economic system, Pakistan seems to have opted for caution rather than excessive innovation. Also, it has concentrated on achieving what are considered to be the main objectives of an Islamic system rather than on using instruments considered purely Islamic. With such an approach, the changes being introduced will be slow and subtle but perhaps permanent. There will probably be few surprises but a great deal of cautious experimentation. The approach, in other words, is pragmatic rather than revolutionary. Despite their similar objectives, therefore, Pakistan is taking a very different route than, for example, Iran or Sudan where Islam has been or is being introduced into economic management with considerable dispatch.

The rest of the Islamic world is watching these experiments with interest. The one in Pakistan is particularly important since a considerable amount of thought has gone into, first, defining what is meant by an Islamic economic system, and then seeking ways gradually to implement it.

NOTES

1. Perhaps the most systematic work on this area is being done by the Islamic Foundation in Islamabad, Pakistan. See the following three publications produced by the

Foundation for views on fiscal and monetary issues: Ziauddin Ahmad, Munawar Iqbal, and M. Fahim Khan, *Fiscal Policy and Resource Allocation in Islam* (1983); Ziauddin Ahmad, Munawar Iqbal, and M. Fahim Khan, *Money and Banking in Islam* (1983); and Munawar Iqbal and M. Fahim Khan, *A Survey of Issues and a Programme for Research in Monetary and Fiscal Economics of Islam* (1981).

2. Government of Pakistan, *Sixth Five-Year Plan: 1983–88* (Islamabad: Planning Commission, 1983).

3. Government of Pakistan, *An Agenda for Islamic Economic Reforms: The Report of the Committee on Islamization Appointed by the Finance Minister* (Islamabad: Pakistan Institute of Development Economics, 1980).

4. Ibid., iii.

5. Ibid., iv.

6. Ibid.

7. Ibid., 8.

8. Ibid., 14.

9. For an evaluation of the impact of the land reforms of 1959 and 1974 on land distribution, see Ronald J. Herring, *Land to the Tiller: Economy of Agrarian Reform in South Asia* (New Haven: Yale University Press, 1983), 85–124.

10. Government of Pakistan, *An Agenda for Islamic Economic Reforms*, 14.

11. Ibid., 8.

12. In his seminal work on the economic development model pursued by Pakistan in the sixties, Gustav Papanek defended the very high rates of profit allowed the private sector on the grounds that since the bulk of these profits were being reinvested, they produced economic growth which was essential for reducing poverty and thereby reducing inequality. See his *Pakistan's Development: Social Goals and Private Incentives* (Cambridge, Massachusetts: Harvard University Press, 1967).

13. Mahbub ul Haq who, as the chief economist of the planning commission, was responsible for much of the thinking embodied in the Second Five-Year Plan, accepted the proposition that "the route to equality lay through inequality" on the ground that during the earlier phase of industrialization such inequality was inevitable. See his *The Strategy of Economic Planning: A Case Study of Pakistan* (Karachi: Oxford University Press, 1963), 32.

14. Government of Pakistan, *An Agenda for Islamic Economic Reforms*, 6.

15. Ibid.

16. See Shahid Javed Burki, *Pakistan under Bhutto, 1971–77* (London: Macmillan, 1980), 122–150 for a discussion of this approach.

17. Mohammad Zia ul-Haq, *Islamic Order—Our Goal: Address to the Nation* (Rawalpindi: Ministry of Information, 1980), 15–16.

18. For a development of this hypothesis, see Shahid Javed Burki, "Pakistan's Sixth Plan: Helping the Country Climb Out of Poverty," *Asian Survey* (April 1985): 400–422.

19. The World Bank, *World Development Report 1984* (Washington, D.C., 1984), 218.

20. Ibid., 226.

21. Ibid., statistical annex, 218–73.

22. Ibid., 254–55.

23. See Shahid Javed Burki, "Developing Countries' Debt: A South Asian Outlook," *Journal of International Affairs* (Summer 1984), 45–60.

4

Islamization and Taxation in Pakistan

Ann Elizabeth Mayer

The payment of the Islamic alms tax, zakat, and its agricultural counterpart, 'ushr, is one of the pillars of the Islamic faith and is theoretically incumbent on all Muslims save the destitute. Until recently, the payment of zakat was a private religious obligation in Pakistan. Because of its private character, the amount distributed as alms by Pakistani Muslims in the past is difficult to estimate. Informal observations suggest, however, that the religious duty to give alms was taken very seriously by a large portion of the populace. In 1979, the Pakistani government decided to convert what had been a duty binding on the believer's conscience into a legal obligation, and undertook the organization of the collection and distribution of the taxes on a national basis.

In this chapter, I assess the changes that the government takeover of zakat has brought to the Pakistani tax system and evaluate their significance both in relation to Islamic law and to their potential impact on the Pakistani economy.

THE PLACE OF THE ZAKAT LAW IN THE PAKISTANI ISLAMIZATION PROGRAM

The process of the Islamization of laws entails different levels of government involvement depending on the kind of Islamic law being imposed. One way of categorizing the differences follows:

1. There can be changes in the wording of legal documents that are basically symbolic in nature, such as the insertion of a constitutional provision making Islam the state religion. Once made, these changes may entail no follow-up measures by the government.
2. There can be legal changes that introduce alterations in existing laws but thereafter entail little government involvement, such as enacting laws substituting Islamic criminal penalties for ones applicable under secular laws, leaving the subsequent application and interpretation of the new rules to the judicial system.
3. There can be changes that not only introduce alterations in existing laws but also require the establishment of new institutions and substantial ongoing government involvement in the implementation and interpretation of the new laws.

Pakistan has experimented with all three kinds of Islamization, but the new zakat law is important in that it belongs in the third category, which involves the kind of legal change that is obviously the most ambitious and costly. It is not surprising, therefore, that many Pakistani officials treat it as the major accomplishment of the Islamization program.

Many Muslims—though by no means all—believe that it is the duty of an Islamic government to collect and distribute the zakat. Therefore, a government that aspires to be viewed as an Islamic government may find it politically desirable to assume this responsibility. Undertaking such a demanding legal reform as part of the Islamization program was one means of establishing the right of the Pakistani regime to claim the title of an Islamic government—meaning, in this case, a government that takes affirmative steps to execute shari'a injunctions, rather than merely a government of a country inhabited by Muslims.

However useful the introduction of zakat may be in shoring up the regime's claim to be ruling in accordance with what some consider to be the requirements of Islamic law, the institution of a compulsory national zakat also involves risks, because it means a government endorsement of one position to the exclusion of others on disputed questions of Islamic doctrine.

Even among Muslims who accept the idea that collecting and distributing zakat is a proper function of a truly Islamic government, there are skeptics who doubt that any of the contemporary regimes in the Muslim world constitutes the kind of Islamic government entitled to collect the zakat. There are Muslims who believe that the zakat must be offered as a voluntary contribution in order to have religious validity—that a compulsory levy imposed by the government is not the test of a Muslim's dedication to the principles of charity and sacrifice that the obligation to pay zakat was meant to be. Many Muslims who are committed to paying the zakat are only willing to turn their contributions over to the leaders and institutions of the particular Islamic sect to which they belong.

Thus, in deciding to enact a law transforming the zakat into a compulsory tax payable to the government, President Zia's regime was requiring many Pakistani Muslims to pay a tax to the government which they, for religious reasons, did not feel that the government was entitled to collect. Negative reactions to the measure, discussed below, exposed the fallacious nature of one of the most fundamental assumptions underlying Islamization programs: that there exists a single, Islamic ideology that enjoys the allegiance of all Muslims. In fact, there are few issues on which there is a consensus as to what Islamic law actually requires, so that government programs officially adopting one particular interpretation of "Islamization" tend to provoke dissent and division. Differences in doctrine affecting zakat liability are naturally particularly contentious, since they have immediate practical financial consequences for both the taxpayers and the recipients of the zakat.

The enactment of the zakat law in Pakistan was a signal that the government was prepared to try to impose its version of Islam in the face of controversy and criticism from Muslims whose views were being implicitly rejected by the adoption of competing norms as the official standard. Concessions belatedly made to dissidents, discussed below, suggested that the government later had second thoughts about the prudence of ignoring the strongly held views of those who disagreed with the official version of the zakat rules.

THE CHARACTER OF THE 1980 PAKISTANI ZAKAT STATUTE

The Pakistani government had various reasons for wanting to find new ways of collecting direct taxes before the zakat law was enacted. Since elements of the federal bureaucracy were allotted a major role in setting up and administering the new Islamic taxes, governmental ideas regarding tax policy and the need for tax reforms have had considerable influence on how the requirements of Islamic taxation have been interpreted. In consequence, aspects of the Islamic taxes ultimately adopted in Pakistan reflect certain governmental priorities and goals for reform of the Pakistani tax system. However, at the same time, in order to have a chance of making the new zakat and 'ushr taxes accepted as religious rather than merely secular tax obligations, some rules going back to the early period of Islamic law had to be retained—rules not necessarily reflecting current economic policies or developmental priorities.

Pakistan's zakat and 'ushr laws, then, melded classical shari'a tax principles and terminology with current governmental taxation goals.

After President Zia inaugurated the Islamization campaign with a speech in February 1979, the Council of Islamic Ideology was given the responsibility of drafting a zakat law. Once the final draft had been approved by the government, a law introducing the new Islamic taxes was enacted. The zakat component of the law took effect in 1981, but implementation of the 'ushr tax was delayed repeatedly until 1983. As a result, there is at present much more data on the former than on the latter tax.

On its face the new law looks like any other statute in Pakistan's contemporary legal system. The obligation to pay the zakat has been transformed by the terms of the new statute from an easily understood religious obligation (and a criterion for distinguishing pious and observant Muslims from hypocritical ones) into something with all the trappings of a very mundane tax liability. Indeed, the taxes due under the new law are linked with features of the regular tax system; for example, the ordinary wealth tax is not levied on assets subject to zakat and the ordinary land revenue is not levied on land or produce subject to 'ushr (Tanzil-ur-Rahman 1981:3). Moreover, the law is replete with bureaucratic technicalities difficult for many Pakistanis, particularly illiterates, to follow.

In this regard, it is instructive to contrast a sampling of Qur'anic injunctions with some representative passages from the new law.

In the Qur'an, it is the religious and moral sensibilities of the believer to which appeal is made. Some examples follow:

> Lo! Those who believe and do good works and establish worship and pay the poor-due, their reward is with their Lord and there shall be no fear come upon them and neither shall they grieve. (2:277)
>
> Those who point at such of the believers as give the alms willingly and such as can find naught to give but their endeavors and deride them—Allah derideth them. Theirs will be a painful doom. (9:79)
>
> Take alms of their wealth, wherewith thou mayst purify them and mayst make them grow, and pray for them. Lo! thy prayer is an assuagement for them. Allah is Hearer, Knower. (9:103)

> Establish worship and pay the poor-due and obey the messenger, that haply ye may find mercy. (24:56)
>
> Lo! those who give alms, both men and women, and lend unto Allah a goodly loan, it will be doubled for them, and theirs will be a rich reward. (57:18)

In the new law, known as the Zakat and 'Ushr Ordinance No. XVII of 1980, the bureaucratic mind has laid down intricate and technical rules recalling the average style of the tax codes and tax regulations familiar to modern taxpayers. Instead of the rich poetry and moral resonance of the Qur'an, the Pakistani taxpayer now encounters the following phraseology:

> Where the recovery of Zakat deductible at source, in respect of any of the assets mentioned in the First Schedule, falls into arrears, the Administrator-General may forward to the Collector of the district concerned a duly signed certificate specifying the amount of arrears due and the particulars of the person from whom due, and the Collector shall, on receipt of such certificate, proceed to recover the amount so specified, as if it were an arrear of land revenue. (Chapter 2, 3. [4])

Or, in the First Schedule, in a listing of assets subject to zakat:

> 8. Securities including shares and debentures of 6 [companies or statutory corporations] excluding those held in the name of an 8 [company or a statutory corporation] and those mentioned at serial number 5, 6, and 7, on which return is payable periodically or otherwise, and is paid.

The rate and basis of zakat assessment on Provident Funds is given in the same schedule as follows:

> 3. In case of non-refundable advance, 2.5% of the amount drawn or, in case of final settlement, 2.5% of the balance standing to the credit of the subscriber as on the Valuation Date, excluding in both cases the employer's contribution and the return accrued thereon.

The change in the conception of the zakat obligation is quite remarkable. There is some question as to whether the religious impulse that ordinarily underlies the payment of zakat will survive its bureaucratization. It would not be surprising if many Pakistanis were to decide that money payable under this law is just like any other tax demanded by the tax authorities of Pakistan. Indeed, in conversations with Pakistanis, I have been told of people who decided that payment of the new tax could not fulfill their religious obligations and therefore felt obliged to continue paying the traditional, private zakat as well as the government zakat. It may be significant in this regard that the voluntary zakat assessments that are also payable to the government under Schedule II of the 1980 law (discussed below) produced only a small percentage of the revenue that government officials originally hoped for, at least in the first years of the new zakat tax.[1] This outcome suggests that where zakat is discretionary, Pakistanis, if they pay zakat, tend not to pay it to the governmental system but to distribute it privately.

This question of what religious significance people will attach to the payment of the governmental zakat also arises in relation to other features of the new law, which has depersonalized the payment of the zakat. In the case of the compulsory zakat, the taxpayer is no longer involved in the payment; instead, the zakat is automatically assessed and deducted on the yearly valuation date by all the institutions holding taxpayer assets subject to the zakat.

The basic distinction between taxable and nontaxable assets under the new zakat law is between enumerated assets in the First Schedule (which must also be held in one of a number of specified Pakistani institutions to be subject to the zakat) and all other forms of wealth, none of which are subject to compulsory zakat under the new laws. (This does not mean, of course, that they are not subject to tax under provisions of other Pakistani tax laws.) This distinction is very different from the one drawn in classical shari'a between hidden *(batin)* and exposed *(zahir)* wealth. Compulsory zakat could be assessed under classical law only against zahir wealth, or specified forms of wealth also exposed to public view. The contrasting category of batin wealth in the classical shari'a comprised assets that were not exposed to public view. There were items of batin wealth that were subject to zakat, but the assessment and payment was left solely to the taxpayer. The notion underlying the zahir/batin distinction was that tax collection should not entail activity by tax assessors that would involve an invasion of the privacy of the taxpayer.

The abandonment of the zahir/batin distinction under the new Pakistani law ties in with a decision to impose the compulsory zakat on forms of wealth very different from those on which the zakat was levied under the classical rules of Islamic law. The classical shari'a rules of taxation, formulated in the first centuries after the death of the Prophet in 632 C.E., quite naturally reflect the main forms of wealth historically found in economies at such early stages of development. Thus, in the classical shari'a, wealth in such forms as precious metals, livestock, and agricultural harvests was taxable. Given this range of taxable assets, the zahir/batin distinction made sense. Items that were subject to the classical zakat are listed only in the Second Schedule appended to the 1980 Pakistani law, where schedules of voluntary taxes to be paid at the option of the taxpayer on various forms of wealth are set forth. The forms of wealth subject to compulsory zakat, the primary focus of the law, are set forth in the First Schedule. Typical First Schedule items include fixed term or savings deposits in banks; shares and debentures—as long as the majority of the shares are owned by Muslims—of various companies; government securities, annuities, and life insurance funds; and funds placed in financial institutions like the National Investment Trust and the Investment Corporation of Pakistan.

The question naturally arises as to whether the Pakistani government's imposition of a mandatory zakat tax on assets like these violates the principle underlying the classical distinction between batin and zahir wealth. The head of the Council of Islamic Ideology and one of the main authors of the draft zakat statute, Justice Tanzil-ur-Rahman, has argued that when people place their assets in banks and other financial institutions, thereby in effect declaring them to the government and placing them under government protection, their money should be treated like zahir wealth. He also asserts that in these circumstances, the assessment of the zakat does not involve the kind of invasion of taxpayer privacy that the classical zahir/batin distinction was meant to prevent (Tanzil-ur-Rahman 1981:21). Others may dispute his analysis, however.

It is instructive to contrast this position with the attitude of the Libyan government. The traditional zahir/batin distinction was retained by Libya when it enacted a zakat statute in the course of its Islamization campaign in the early seventies.[2] At that time, Libya enjoyed more revenue from its oil than its tiny population and undeveloped economy could absorb. It did not need to increase tax revenue; therefore the fact that most private wealth was classified as batin and immune from compulsory levies under the national zakat did not deprive the state of needed funds. Since the purpose of the Libyan zakat law was to demonstrate the fidelity of the revolutionary regime to Islamic principles—not to raise tax revenues—it is not surprising that the Libyan law more closely replicates features of the traditional shari'a rules than does the Pakistani law.[3] In Pakistan, the zakat tax is meant to be a revenue-producing measure.

THE PAKISTANI TAX SYSTEM

It is important to have a general picture of the Pakistani tax system in order to appreciate the nature of the changes called for by the new Islamic taxes.

One way to evaluate a country's tax system is to measure the size of the actual revenue yield in comparison with the taxable capacity of the country (Toye 1978:5). By this measure, Pakistan is a country with a relatively poor tax base and a relatively low tax yield in relation to its actual capacity (Prest 1978:21).

There is a widespread view that Pakistan's tax laws are basically antiquated and in need of revision. The system depends heavily on indirect and regressive taxes (e.g., customs duties and sales taxes) and does not effectively reach the wealth and incomes of the richest individuals and companies. Achieving a modern and less regressive tax system will require a shift to direct taxation in which individuals and companies bear tax burdens more proportionate to their incomes and wealth. However, while indirect taxes are relatively easy to administer, preconditions for an effective system of direct taxes include a sophisticated infrastructure capable of monitoring taxpayer compliance, trustworthy and comprehensive systems of accounting and record-keeping, and a high degree of taxpayer cooperation. Pakistan lacks these factors, and tax reform designed to achieve a greater measure of direct taxation has so far proved difficult.

The failure to achieve a more effective system of direct taxation is partly due to several factors that make tax evasion relatively easy in Pakistan.

One factor handicapping the Pakistani tax authorities in their attempts to ferret out tax evasion is the fact that they do not have the elaborate computer systems to assist in identifying tax fraud and delinquency that are available to the Internal Revenue Service in the United States.

Another factor is that while in the United States 90 percent of transactions are made by check or credit card, in Pakistan almost all transactions are made on a cash basis, so there are few records which tax authorities can check to establish the true income of individuals or businesses. Unlike U.S. businesses, most Pakistani businesses are run by families, and details of company finances are generally kept as family secrets. Outsiders have no means of access to the real business records of such companies, which often keep two sets of books, one being specially prepared to understate earnings and to mislead any probing tax authorities. Accountants in Pakistan, unlike those in the United States, have not so far been held liable in suits for damages by third parties who have been injured by fraudulent company accounts prepared by them. Pakistani accountants may rely for their accounts on whatever information a company gives them, without fear of liability if that information proves to have been misleading to investors.

The failure of Pakistani tax authorities to collect the tax revenues legally due from the private sector is conceded by officials, as in public comments made by Finance Secretary H. U. Beg (Zubeiri 1984:12). In extensive discussions with a wide range of Pakistanis in the course of research in Islamabad, Karachi, and Lahore in 1982, I found general confirmation of the view that income tax evasion had become a national pastime. Revenue recovery from direct taxes remains very low despite the fact that Pakistani income tax rates are quite high—rising to levels of 60 percent for individuals in the highest bracket and 65 percent for private companies. These high rates may themselves have been counterproductive. A number of the people whom I interviewed professed to see a connection between the officially high and progressive rates of taxation and widespread tax evasion; individuals and businesses were determined to conceal their real incomes to avoid what they considered to be exorbitant tax demands.

Given all this, one could argue that the zakat tax, in its bureaucratic conception as a flat-rate levy on certain types of assets held in institutions that do keep records (allowing the extent of any taxable holdings to be determined), was a tax measure well-suited to overcoming some of the problems afflicting the Pakistani tax system.

The zakat tax rate is a flat 2.5 percent and the 'ushr rate a flat 5 or 10 percent, depending on certain conditions; both correspond to the rates set in classical Islamic law.

The flat rate embodied in the Pakistani Islamic tax models may be on the verge of adoption in other areas. The government seems to have come round to the idea that it will actually increase tax revenues by resorting to flat rate taxes on income even if these are set far below current income tax rates. Indeed, the Pakistani finance minister in 1983 offered a bargain to the nonagricultural sectors of the economy: he would abolish income tax and corporation tax as long as these sectors agreed to comply with a flat rate 5 percent tax like that applied under the 'ushr law.[4]

FEATURES OF THE PAKISTANI ZAKAT TAX

Under the 1980 Pakistani law the zakat tax is assessed annually against Muslim citizens of Pakistan who have had at least Rs. 2,000 worth of certain kinds of assets at some time during the tax year.

It is also assessed against companies and other associations (whether incorporated or not) in which the major portion of shares or beneficial ownership is held by Muslim citizens of Pakistan (Chapter 1.1.[2]). This measure constitutes a considerable change from the classical shari'a, where only individual persons were subject to the zakat. Islamic law did not recognize companies as juristic persons or provide for a corporate form of doing business. The extension of the zakat levy to companies is in keeping with the tendency in the Pakistani law to depersonalize the zakat obligation and to move away from interpreting it as a test of personal piety and virtue—seeing it instead as a vehicle for enhancing public revenue and funding a social security system.

As specified in the Qur'an, the purposes for which the zakat is to be used are quite diverse, subsidizing the needy being only one of them: "The alms are for the poor and the needy, and those who collect them [the tax collectors], and those whose hearts are to be reconciled [for mitigating the hostility of enemies of the early Muslim community], to free the captives [or slaves, in some interpretations] and the debtors, for the cause of Allah [including the *jihad* (holy war), in many interpretations], and for the wayfarer" (Qur'an 9:60).

Given this original range of uses for the zakat, the interpretation of it in the modern Pakistani law as providing a safety net for the needy amounts to a distinct narrowing of its traditional purpose. This narrowing of purpose does not seem to have provoked much criticism; it seems that most Pakistanis had already come to think of zakat as alms for the needy—as a kind of informal, private welfare system—before the government intervened to take it over as a national welfare system.

It is interesting that the tax is assessed not just against the assets of adults but against those of children as well. This rule has been adopted despite the fact that under the rules of Hanafi fiqh—the dominant legal school in Pakistan—only the assets of adults should be subject to the zakat levy. The rule allowing minors to be taxed was borrowed from the rules of the Maliki and Shafi'i schools, which otherwise have had little influence on Islamic jurisprudence in Pakistan. The rules of these schools were preferred on this point in recognition of the Pakistani predilection for exploiting all means of tax evasion. Had the zakat not been imposed on the assets of minors, it was believed, adult taxpayers would have resorted to fraudulent transfers of assets to minors to shield themselves from tax liability.[5]

The selection of which assets would be subject to the compulsory zakat was made on the basis of where accurate institutional records existed and what would maximize administrative convenience while minimizing the costs of assessment and collection.

The assets chosen were those that were so placed that the task and costs of collecting the zakat could be passed onto banks, other financial institutions, and companies. Irfan Ahmad Imtiyazi, the chief zakat administrator, explained in an interview on 13 March 1982, that this arrangement was chosen because government members believed that assessment and collection of the zakat had to be carried out virtually cost-free. If, instead, considerable administrative overhead had to be paid out of zakat funds, people could resist payment of the zakat to the government on the grounds that a greater percentage of their alms would reach the intended beneficiaries if they continued to pay the zakat directly to the recipients in the traditional manner. According to Imtiyazi, even his own salary was charged to general government funds rather than against the zakat revenue.

The concern to ensure that Pakistan's zakat funds are not depleted by administrative charges is interesting in the light of the fact that the Qur'an (9:60) specifically provides that zakat funds are to be used to pay those who collect the taxes. (As noted, the Qur'anic principles for use of the zakat have not been followed in all cases in determining zakat recipients under the Pakistanti law.) In declining to finance the administration of the zakat out of zakat revenues, the law seems to reflect an acute awareness of and pragmatic accommodation to the attitudes of the average Pakistani taxpayer, who is ready to seize on any pretext to justify refusing to pay taxes to the government. However, one can ask whether the cost-free administration of the zakat is only an illusion. Will not the institutions which do bear the costs of assessing and collecting the zakat ultimately pass on their costs to the consumer/taxpayer? It would seem that they must do so, but the link between these added costs and the zakat system is apparently regarded as too remote to attract the taxpayers' notice.

TAX POLICY IN DEVELOPING ECONOMIES AND IN THE PAKISTANI ECONOMY

Pakistan has a mixed economy in which both the public and private sectors play important roles. Tax policy can be used to shape economic development in the private sector of the economy. Like other developing countries, Pakistan has to be concerned about two basic goals in formulating its tax policies: promotion of economic growth and improvement in the distribution of income. A critical function of taxation in a developing economy is to inhibit private consumption while encouraging savings.

Other important considerations in creating a tax policy include ease and efficiency in administering a tax system to keep overheads low and attaining a standard of enforcement which maximizes revenue while minimizing evasion and inequity (Toye 1978:3–5; Due 1976:77–79). In some ways the new zakat tax seems ideally suited to development needs, while in other respects its impact may be more problematic.

While it is possible that the zakat law might give some people the incentive to purchase consumer items not taxable under zakat rules, it seems unlikely that such a low tax will significantly change buying patterns. In this respect the introduction of the zakat seems neither a plus nor a minus in terms of its effect on economic development.

The relatively heavy burden borne by the small saver has provoked criticism on the grounds of inequity. One aspect of the system that has been criticized is that current accounts, in which large businesses may have considerable sums, are not subject to the zakat, resulting in a relatively light tax burden. In contrast, the bite from the zakat tax is disproportionately severe for poor individuals, whose assets are unlikely to be in current accounts and are taxed at the same flat rate as those of the rich. Only accounts with less than Rs. 2,000—about $140 at current rates—are exempted from the zakat levy. In response to public criticism of such inequities, the government doubled the minimum amount subject to zakat, which was originally set at only Rs. 1,000. However, many people feel that the minimum taxable amount should be still higher.

The classical shari'a did provide that only persons possessing a certain minimum amount, known as the *nisab*, needed to pay the zakat. It is difficult to compare amounts discussed in medieval treatises with the minimum amounts of wealth subject to the zakat under the Pakistani law due to the intervening economic transformations and the fact that very different kinds of wealth are taxable under the Pakistani law. Thus, purely as a matter of shari'a law, it is difficult to establish exactly what the proper nisab should be in a modern economy or whether the minimum amount has been set too low under the Pakistani law.

Aside from the question of equity, there is another problem with the levy of the zakat on the assets of small savers. Such a levy on savings potentially deters saving, thus flouting the accepted wisdom among development economists that a developing country should provide every possible incentive to small savers to keep all of their surplus funds in savings accounts where they can be mobilized for productive investment.

Any possible deterrent effect that the zakat tax might have on small savers would be a serious disadvantage in Pakistan, which, more than most countries, needs to find ways of raising its savings rate. The savings rate, quite low for a developing country, has hovered around 5 to 7 percent in recent years, while many other developing countries have attained rates of up to 20 percent.[6]

In terms of ease and efficiency of administration, the current Pakistani zakat system seems to perform extremely well. It therefore meets the developmental economics criterion that taxation costs should be kept as low as possible.

Regarding the criterion of minimizing tax evasion, the success of the Pakistani zakat law is less certain. It is feasible to evade all or part of the zakat simply by not keeping one's assets in forms taxable under the zakat law or by removing assets from the taxing instituions just before the assessment is made on the first day of Ramadan. Since people do not have to record their real reasons for placing, withdrawing, or transferring funds, no reliable data exist on the number of taxpayers who have attempted such tax dodges. Informal sources suggest however, that while many people may have attempted to shift assets in 1981 when the tax was first introduced, fewer have done so since. In any event, it is obviously risky, inconvenient, and costly to withdraw funds just before Ramadan every year from savings accounts, fixed term accounts, mutual funds, investments in securities, life insurance policies, and the like. It is no coincidence, one assumes, that the choice of assets on which the zakat is levied is such as to discourage withdrawals made to evade the tax.

In this connection, one should consider the significance of the fact that the valuation date for calculating the zakat is the first day of Ramadan, the holy month of fasting. This is a date on which a believer's religious feelings are likely to be intensified by the pious atmosphere and ceremony attendant on inaugurating the month of fasting. If taxpayers accept the government's claims that the restructured zakat is a religious obligation, religious sentiment may deter them from withdrawing funds to avoid tax on the assessment date.

EXEMPTIONS FROM THE ZAKAT AND SUNNI-SHI'A DIFFERENCES

Exemptions from the zakat on the basis of sectarian differences have presented problems. The imposition of the compulsory zakat brought to the fore an issue which advocates of Islamization try to suppress or downplay. It concerns the problems created by enacting an official version of Islamic law in the face of differences of opinion among members of different schools and sects as to what Islam requires. The late Maulana Maududi, the most prominent among the advocates of Islamization in Pakistan, deprecated the significance of what he called "the bogey of sectarian differences" as a barrier to the readoption of Islamic law as the law of the land in Pakistan. In Maududi's view, while Muslims whose views were in the minority were entitled—like members of non-Muslim minorities—to follow their own laws in personal status matters, in other matters they were bound by whatever version of the shari'a was enacted into law with the approval of the majority. The members of Muslim minority communities would, he argued, prefer to follow the Islamic law of another sect rather than to see Pakistan's "un-Islamic" laws continue (Maududi 1975:62–64).The Pakistani zakat tax law as originally enacted was meant to apply to all Pakistani Muslims. However, the government underestimated the strength of the opposition to the new tax by members of the Shi'a community.

The Pakistani Islamization program, in which the influence of followers of Maududi and conservative Sunni mullahs has been prominent, has not won favor with Shi'a leaders. Their views on what Islamic law requires have not been shown much deference by President Zia's regime. Their followers, who number between 10 percent and 30 percent of the population depending on the source one uses, were persuaded that they were entitled to resist the compulsory zakat payment. Shi'a leaders claimed that it violated the right of Shi'as to distribute alms as dictated by their consciences and in accordance with the guidelines of Islamic law as interpreted in the jurisprudence of their own sect. Protests and an enormous mass demonstration in Islamabad by Shi'as followed the promulgation of the zakat law. While the focus of Shi'a grievances was the requirement that they submit to the compulsory zakat, some Pakistanis claim that the real impetus behind the demonstrations was the Shi'as' growing political alienation from the policies of the martial law regime. The zakat law, in this view, merely provided a pretext and a rallying point for such disaffection.

In 1981, the government finally decided to give way and allow persons who objected to paying the compulsory zakat for jurisprudential reasons to file for exemptions from the tax. On 27 April 1981, the Ministry of Finance issued a Notification allowing Shi'as to claim an exemption on the basis of fiqh from the governmental zakat. This could be done by filing an attested true copy of a declaration on a form CZ-50 with a Zakat Deduction Office "within three months preceding the Valuation Date." However, renewed controversy erupted in 1982, the next tax year, when many Shi'as belatedly discovered that, in the absence of a timely filing of a second form CZ-50, their assets were being treated as subject to the zakat.

This requirement of a fresh application for a fiqh-based exemption in each tax year struck many as peculiar, since it is highly unusual for Muslims to change sectarian affiliation. In addition, many people did not become aware of the additional filing requirement until after the deadline for filing exemption applications had passed. The form CZ-50 had to be filed by 25 March 1982, even though Ramadan did not start until late June, and there were complaints that this filing date had not been adequately advertised. The result was an exacerbation of bad feeling in Shi'a communities and suspicions that the earlier concession of an exemption for Shi'as had been illusory. Subsequent violent Sunni-Shi'a confrontations revealed growing sectarian tensions. These may be traceable in some measure to the polarization encouraged by the reactions and counterreactions to the zakat law.

In any event, the experiences of the Shi'a community have led to a situation where a sizeable segment of the population is more than ever determined to resist the governmental zakat as a matter of religious principle.

NON-MUSLIMS AND THE ZAKAT

A more complex issue is the impact that the zakat tax will have on the status of non-Muslim Pakistanis. While one hardly expects protests from groups exempted from tax liability, the fact that the zakat is levied only on Muslims may add to the growing sense of many non-Muslim Pakistanis that Islamization is slowly making them second-class citizens. Just as the exemption of Israel's Arab population from military service symbolizes the Arabs' status as an out-group, so the exemption of Pakistan's non-Muslims from the zakat tax may be taken as a sign that adherence to Islam is becoming the real basis of political community in the country. It is one sign among many that in the era of Islamization, Pakistan may be moving away from the vision articulated by Muhammad Ali Jinnah in his Presidential Address on 11 August 1947: a vision of a country where all citizens would enjoy equality regardless of religious affiliation.

THE 'USHR TAX

Although the 'ushr tax was covered in the 1980 law, it was not applied until 1983. It seems that the delay was due to official recognition that it was potentially problematic in its economic impact. The classical shari'a tax rules were, after all, originally developed and applied in societies at a very early stage of economic development, in which crops were a major source of wealth. It was then natural to subject crops to higher tax rates than other assets.

The Pakistani 'ushr law, in emulation of the classical shari'a rules, imposes a 5 percent tax on the value of harvests on artificially irrigated land and a 10 percent tax on the value of harvests on agricultural lands that do not have artificial irrigation. Although Pakistani agriculture has been doing well, no Pakistani official with whom I spoke was able to identify a principle of developmental economics that would warrant the imposition of such taxes on Pakistani agriculture at this stage. Thus, the impetus behind the imposition of the 'ushr seems to be the government's desire to revive Islamic law rather than any of the practical considerations that encouraged the prompt adoption of and levying of the zakat.

Many rules affecting 'ushr are scattered throughout sections of the 1980 law, but most are concentrated in Chapter 3. It says there that the 'ushr is to be collected "from every landowner, grantee, allottee, leasee, leaseholder, or land-holder" for any crops grown on their land. Exempted are those who are needy enough to be eligible to receive zakat, or whose wheat crops weigh less than 948 kilograms or are worth less than the value of such a wheat crop. The tax is to be paid in cash on a self-assessment basis under the supervision of a local committee empowered to review the accuracy of taxpayers' assessments. This system seems much less certain to produce accurate and consistent tax assessments than the institutionally-based zakat assessment system.

The ordinary land revenue tax, known as the *malia*, is not to be levied on any land or harvest subject to the 'ushr. Moreover, the government decided that, just as the classical shari'a rules reduced the 'ushr liability of the farmer whose land was irrigated by artificial methods—which are assumed to require human effort and expense to build and maintain—so a portion of the expenses that a Pakistani farmer incurs to improve his crop yields by such means as fertilizers and insecticides should be applied to reduce his 'ushr liability.[7] That such tax deductions are being allowed suggests a tacit acknowledgment that the classical 'ushr rates are too high in the context of Pakistan's modern economy.

The readjustments in the 'ushr rates prompt consideration of questions that will occur to anyone familiar with the role of modern governments in the agricultural sector. To what extent is a "tax" on agriculture meaningful in a situation where agricultural income, prices, costs, and inputs are products of government agricultural policies and centralized planning, and where what is grown, how much is grown, and how large individual agricultural holdings are are determined by the same government that imposes the "tax"? In Pakistan, as in most modern countries, the government intervenes extensively in the agricultural sector of the economy, and it would be unusual if, once having settled the details of agricultural policy, it did not intervene again when a new tax was imposed to redress any resulting imbalances in the system. This situation, where agricultural production and income are artificially fixed by the government, is markedly different from the one contemplated by the jurists who devised the classical shari'a rules. They lived in an era when agricultural production and income were determined by market forces rather than by the same government that would be taxing the harvests. It is questionable whether the rationale for the agricultural levies imposed in typical ancient and medieval economies make sense when transferred to the agricultural sectors of modern economies, and it is quite possible that the effects of the Pakistani 'ushr tax will be cancelled out by subsequent readjustments in the system.

CONCLUSION

The introduction of Islamic taxation in Pakistan represents an important experiment in making Pakistani law more Islamic while also attempting to accommodate shari'a principles to current economic realities and development policies. While the economic impact of the 'ushr tax is uncertain, the zakat tax is in many respects well-designed to fit the goals of Pakistani tax policy. On balance, despite its drawbacks, the zakat law may increase government revenues and be a useful tax reform from the standpoint of government economic priorities. However, the religious and political implications of the decision to impose a Sunni version of Islamic taxes in a country that has both Muslim minority sects and non-Muslim minorities are complex and far-reaching. It is premature at this stage to try to predict the consequences of the zakat law for the future of Islamic law in Pakistan and for the concept of Pakistani nationhood, but both issues merit further attention. The results of the Pakistani experiment with Islamic taxes may also have important lessons for other governments contemplating a program of Islamization.

NOTES

1. Interview with Irfan Ahmad Imtiyazi, Secretary of the Ministry of Religious and Minorities Affairs and Administrator-General of the Central Zakat Council, on 13 March 1982.

2. See Law 89 of 28 October 1971 and the decision of the Council of Ministers of 15 February 1972.

3. Of course, Qadhafi's subsequent imposition of his radical Green Book theories has all but obliterated private property, rendering the zahir/batin distinction virtually meaningless.

4. "A Roundtable with Dr. Mahbubul Haq." *Pakistan and Gulf Economic Digest* (2–8 July 1983):12–23.

5. Interview with Justice Tanzil-ur-Rahman on 17 March 1982, and Tanzil-ur-Rahman (1981:22–23).

6. "Advice from the Central Bank." *Pakistan and Gulf Economic Digest* (31 December 1983–6 January 1984):7; Zubeiri 1984:11.

7. Interview with Javaid Azfar on 15 July 1982.

REFERENCES

Aghnides, Nicholas P. n.d. *Mohammedan Theories of Finance.* Lahore: Premier Book House.

Due, John F. 1976. "Value-Added Taxation in Developing Countries." In *Taxation and Development*, edited by Nian-Tzu Wang. New York: Praeger.

Enthoven, Adolf J. H. 1977. *Accountancy Systems in Third World Economies.* Amsterdam: North Holland.

Government of Pakistan. n.d. *Pakistan Economic Survey 1981–82.* Islamabad: Government Publications.

Harriss, C. Lowell. 1976. "Property Taxation and Development." In *Taxation and Development*, edited by Nian-Tzu Wang. New York: Praeger.

Laishley, Roy, Jonathan Friedland, and a special correspondent. 1984. "Sudan—Nimairi Tests Donors' Patience." *African Economic Digest* (June 8):2–3.

al-Marghinani, Burhan al-Din. 1975. *The Hedaya.* Translated by Charles Hamilton. Lahore: Premier Book House.

Maududi, Abul A'la. 1975. *The Islamic Law and Constitution.* Lahore: Islamic Publications.

Prest, A. R. 1978. "The Taxable Capacity of a Country." In *Taxation and Economic Development*, edited by J. F. J. Toye. London: Cass.

Rodinson, Maxime. 1966. *Islam et Capitalisme.* Paris: Seuil.

Tanzil-ur-Rahman. 1981. *Introduction of Zakat in Pakistan.* Islamabad: Council of Islamic Ideology.

Toye, J. F. 1978. "Introduction: Taxation and Economic Development: Answers and Questions from Recent Research." In *Taxation and Economic Development*, edited by J. F. Toye. London: Cass.

Zubeiri, Khalique. 1984. "No Simple Answers to Vital Economic Questions." *Pakistan and Gulf Economic Digest* (7–13 January):11–13.

Other Sources:

Interviews with a wide range of officials of the Pakistani government, lawyers, intellectuals, journalists, bankers, educators, and religious leaders during research trips to Pakistan in March and July through August, 1982.

5

Pakistan's Zakat and 'Ushr as a Welfare System

Grace Clark

Pakistan's zakat and 'ushr system comprises an essential part of the Islamization program of the current government. Shortly after coming to power, General Zia ul-Haq emphasized the need to establish zakat in an Islamic state (Zia ul-Haq 1979). In introducing the zakat system in 1980, he called it "an essential pillar of Islam's welfare system." The preamble to the Zakat and 'Ushr Ordinance (1980) states that "the prime objective of the collection of zakat and 'ushr, and disbursements therefrom, is to assist the needy, the indigent and the poor." As organized in Pakistan, zakat combines elements of Islam's traditional religious welfare institution with those of a modern public welfare system. The moral imperative and much of the specific format are directly based on the Qur'an and the shari'a. The system establishes the nation as the unit of policy and as the body authorized to collect and distribute zakat: based on national law, it uses currency as the basic medium of assistance, bases eligibility on individual need, and is administered through a government bureaucracy.

This chapter examines Pakistan's zakat and 'ushr system as an operating welfare system, or "a system for providing a means of livelihood to those who cannot earn their own living by means considered normal in the community" (Pusic 1971). It describes how Pakistan's zakat works "on the ground" and explores some issues now facing the system.

Data for this chapter were collected in over two hundred interviews throughout Pakistan from October 1983 to March 1984 and through subsequent correspondence with key officials in the zakat system, with members of various levels of zakat committees, with *mustahaqeen*, and with people outside the zakat system. Additional data were obtained from responses to a mail-out questionnaire to a random sample of local zakat committees.

BACKGROUND OF PAKISTAN'S SYSTEM

Zakat is one of the five pillars of Islam, the acts required of a Muslim to demonstrate submission to God. Its primary traditional function is as an act of piety. It also reinforces the responsibility of Muslims for each other's physical and social well-being.

Zakat as a traditional religious institution involves both the payment and distribution of zakat. Muslim jurists have defined zakat as a "complete, unilateral, and unconditional transfer by a Muslim of ownership, with all its usufructs, as an act of piety of a prescribed portion of property to a poor Muslim, other than a member of Hashimi Sajid family [a relative of the Prophet], if he owns more than the prescribed wealth as laid down by shari'a" (Tanzil-ur-Rahman 1980). Essentially, zakat is payment by a Muslim who has more than enough wealth to meet his needs (a *sahib-e-nisab*), to one of certain kinds of deserving poor Muslims (mustahaqeen).

As traditionally interpreted by Hanafi fiqh, zakat is to be paid once a year during the holy month of Ramadan on wealth held more than a year (Maududi 1980). Zakat rates vary with the amount of labor, degree of risk, and degree of good fortune involved in producing the wealth. Generally, the zakat rate is 2½ percent on, for example, money, gold, or silver, while it is 20 percent on the produce of mines. There is an elaborate schedule of rates for animals, depending on the species, age, and sex of the animal (Aghnides 1981).

Traditionally, too, zakat is paid only to certain groups, or "heads," specified in the Qur'an and shari'a. These are the poor (with no income); the needy (with some income, but not enough to support themselves); recent converts to Islam; those in debt through circumstances beyond their control; travelers; slaves to be emancipated; those who collect and disburse zakat; and those who do the good works of God (Maududi 1980; Aghnides 1981). The Qur'an exhorts over a hundred times that Muslims should give zakat. It particularly emphasizes giving zakat to those who are poor and to needy widows and orphans. In Hanafi tradition, the concept of *tamlik* requires zakat to be given as an absolute gift to one individual or for his use.

'Ushr is another form of almsgiving paid on the produce of land exceeding the value of 948 kilograms of wheat. It is not a tax on the value of the land itself, but on the harvest, and is due after each harvest. If the harvest is lost for any reason, no 'ushr is due. As 'ushr is a part of the religious tradition of almsgiving, the term *zakat* as used throughout this chapter will be assumed to include 'ushr.

Zakat is an integral part of Islamic history; it was established by the Prophet himself as part of the administrative structure of his government. After the Prophet's death, two tribes north of Medina which had previously paid zakat to the Prophet refused to pay zakat to his successor, Abu Bakr. Abu Bakr went to war against them to establish the principle that they must pay zakat to him as the legitimate representative of the Prophet's authority. Abu Bakr also introduced a guaranteed minimum standard of income, granting each man, woman, and child ten dirhams annually; this was later increased to twenty dirhams (Sharif 1979). The next two caliphs, Omar and Usman, continued to codify and clarify zakat. During the caliphate of 'Ali, the payment of zakat became embroiled in the issue of the legitimacy of the government. After 'Ali's death, his followers (later known as Shi'as) refused to pay zakat to his successor because they did not recognize the government's legitimacy (Aghnides 1981).

Zakat as a governmental structure in an Islamic state had its last days during the reign of Umar bin Abdul Aziz (717–20 A.D.). It is reported that during his reign, no one could be found in Medina who needed zakat (Tanzil-ur-Rahman 1981). This report is often cited today as the epitome of a system which identifies zakat with a time of enormous political power and prosperity for Muslims, and social and economic justice for all. For centuries after 720 A.D., zakat was considered an individual responsibility and act of devotion.

Shi'as, comprising a sizable minority of Pakistan's Muslims, traditionally pay zakat by setting aside 5 percent of all incoming wealth throughout the year, paying it both to the poor directly and to their religious teachers (who are more hierarchically organized than those of the Sunni majority). Unlike the Hanafi understanding of tamlik, the Shi'as hold that projects benefitting the whole communty fall within the category of "good works of Allah." According to long-standing Shi'a doctrine, no government has the right to collect zakat unless it is the legitimate successor to the Prophet, which no modern government has been construed to be. Thus, while both Sunni and Shi'a Pakistani Muslims agree on the importance of zakat as a pillar of Islam, they differ fundamentally on how zakat should be determined, who may collect it, and how it may be used.

In the twentieth century, two overlapping sets of South Asian Muslim intellectuals have elaborated and reinforced a vision of zakat as an integral part of the socioeconomic system of an ideal Islamic state. The first group are the "ideological engineers, who are striving to develop an Islamic identity that is totally Muslim and totally relevant to the modern world" (Haddad 1982). Represented most articulately by Maulana Maududi in Pakistan, this group has exerted a strong influence on the policies of the Pakistani government since its founding. The second group are the Islamic economists, led by Shaikh Mahmud Ahmad who, as early as 1947, published *The Economics of Islam*, in which he presented Islam as a systematic socioeconomic alternative to both capitalism and socialism. For this group, a very traditional interpretation of zakat provides the underpinning for an envisioned perfect Islamic society. Both groups see zakat as serving the Islamic state as a social security system, providing comfortable levels of support for those in need.

More recent Muslim economists have built on traditional concepts of zakat while exploring new dimensions of these concepts. Naqvi (1981) sets out an important role for zakat in establishing economic and social justice through the redistribution of wealth. Khurshid Ahmad (1983) identifies a key role for zakat in economic development, which would raise not only the well-being of individuals but also of the whole society.

Events of the 1970s and 1980s have provided enormous energy to these visions. Large numbers of people throughout the Muslim world have become convinced that an Islamic system, with zakat as the main source of revenue collection, can produce economic justice, provide a social security system, eliminate poverty and beggary, rehabilitate the poor to self-sufficiency, and increase the total wealth and well-being of the larger society. Political leaders throughout the Islamic world have fueled this vision: inclusion of at least some mention of zakat has become something of an Islamic litmus test to determine whether or not a government is "Islamic."

While tremendous expectations have accrued to zakat, Naqvi and others in *An Agenda for Islamic Economic Reform* (1980) warn that zakat alone, and especially a partial implementation of the zakat system, should not be expected to bring about these economic goals singlehandedly.

Although many people wax romantic about how Muslims have always paid zakat and how voluntary zakat can achieve economic justice, the most rapid glance at Pakistan's social structure documents the prevalence of poverty there. People may recall their own parents and grandparents as generous with zakat, but severe disparities in wealth have existed for centuries. Traditional zakat practices certainly helped some people, but such help was ad hoc, irregular, a function of the number of rich people in a particular village, inequitable, and dependent on the donor's individual interpretation of his religious responsibility.

Although little research has been done on personal zakat practices, a study made by Sabzwari in 1978 among middle-class educated Muslims in a subdivision of Karachi shows that while almost all (95 percent) had heard of zakat, fewer than one-fourth paid zakat regularly themselves. Only about 5 percent had ever heard of 'ushr.

As Pakistan changes from a traditional to a more industrialized and urban society, it is finding (as did the West) that traditional charities and family networks, however well-intentioned, are overwhelmed by the scope of economic change and its consequences. The state is the only organized institutional vehicle with sufficient authority, scope, and resources to orchestrate nationwide solutions to poverty (Wilensky and Lebeaux 1965; Flora and Heidenheimer 1981), for while development schemes set out to upgrade groups of people, segments of the economy, or the society as a whole, it is government welfare systems which address the immediate subsistence needs of individual persons.

In 1978, President Zia asked the Council of Islamic Ideology to address, theoretically, the issue of a zakat system in Pakistan. Shortly after that, he appointed a task group headed by H. U. Beg (then in the Planning Ministry and now secretary in the Finance Ministry) to formulate a plan to fund and implement a zakat system. In March 1979, President Zia appointed I. A. Imtiyazi, a career administrator with a strong reputation for personal integrity, to begin to set up the system. It had to have an effective collection system falling within the guidelines of the shari'a, but administratively simple enough to minimize the cost of collection and prevent its being bogged down in minutiae, loopholes, or appeals. Eligibility was to be determined on the precepts of the shari'a, but also had to be simple, equitable, and sensible. Given Pakistan's historical experience with tax evasion and graft, the new system had to have strong accountability mechanisms so that people could believe in its integrity. Finally, since the system was to be based on Islamic precepts and was to use those precepts to draw upon resources, it had to be credible: to meet the "Islamic expectations" of the people and the government.

PAKISTAN'S SYSTEM "ON THE GROUND"

Conceptually, Pakistan's zakat system is very simple. Most zakat is deducted at the source from financial institutions, forwarded to the Central Zakat Fund, and disbursed through Provincial Zakat Funds to a nationwide network of local zakat committees. These committees determine eligibility and give out grants to mustahaqeen. In rural areas, the local zakat committee also determines 'ushr and supervises its collection, adding these funds to those received from provincial disbursements. (It should be noted that 'ushr has not been as successful in its implementation as has zakat.) Voluntary contributions are also added to the local zakat committee's account. Simple in concept, zakat becomes a much more complex system in actual implementation.

As our primary concern in this chapter is with zakat as a social welfare system, our focus is on the administrative aspects of the distribution of monies to mustahaqeen, and the effects of this distribution.

The administrative structure of zakat, consisting of a blend of highly professional civil servants and unpaid volunteers, is actually two parallel systems. At each level of government, volunteers, organized in committees, make policy decisions appropriate for that level and are integrally involved in the day-to-day functioning of the system. At the local level, volunteers comprise the large body of workers who carry out the actual work of zakat—eligibility determination, disbursement of zakat, records keeping, and, in many instances, collection of 'ushr. Paid staff are used to implement the policies formulated by the volunteers. They support the volunteer system, using their technical and administrative expertise—as well as their authority—to help the volunteers make the system work.

The volunteer system is internally hierarchical, that is, each level of the system is directly accountable to the next higher level. The professional staff is quasi-hierarchical; it coordinates with the professional zakat staff of the next higher level of government and also has line accountability through the governmental structure at the same level of government. The local-level professional staff accounts directly to the local zakat committee. The professional and volunteer staffs interface at each level of government, with at least one member of the professional staff serving as part of the volunteer committee at each level except the local.

As in most welfare systems, the functions of the administrative structure differ at each governmental level. The Central Zakat Committee carries the primary responsibility for formulating policy guidelines, while the Administrator General Zakat and his staff put these into appropriate governmental format and disseminate them. In contrast, a local zakat committee makes little formal policy, but carries the brunt of actual operations. The proportion of effort a committee devotes to policy versus operational decisions decreases with each level of government.

All staff filling national and provincial policy-making posts are ap-

FIGURE 5.1.
System of Collection and Distribution of Zakat and 'Ushr in Pakistan.

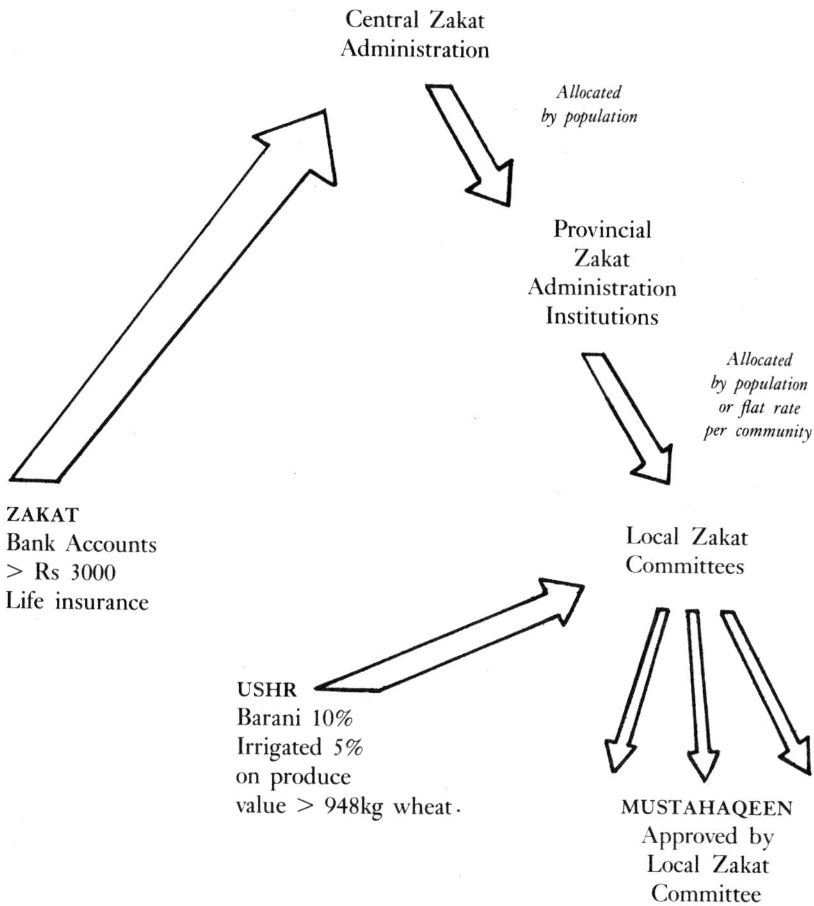

pointed. At the national level, they are appointed by the president; as the policy-making function diminishes with each level, the proportion of committee members elected to their posts rises until, at the level of the Local Zakat Committee, all are elected locally, and in turn elect their own chairman.

This administrative structure involves large numbers of people: as of 10 January 1983, there were 37,033 local zakat committees with 7 members each, for a total of 259,241 people. Adding in 289 *tehsil* (sub-district), 72 district, and 4 provincial committees, zakat's administration involves more than 275,000 people in all (according to the General Zakat Administration in 1983).

Communication is often a major logistical exercise, especially since many villages do not contain a telephone. Moreover, the Central Zakat Administration estimates that half of the members of local zakat committees are illiterate and that a quarter of the committees, especially in rural areas, do not have any member who is literate. Policy is communicated, verbally and in writing, down both the parallel hierarchies. At the district and tehsil levels, this is usually accomplished through meetings. However, policy is often also disseminated from the district level by mail, directly to both tehsil and local committees. To reinforce policy consistency and to provide moral support to the volunteer committees, the Central Zakat Administration sends out a monthly magazine, *al-Zakat*, which contains inspirational articles, news of volunteer committee accomplishments, and articles on policy changes. Because policy dissemination and report compilation has been hampered by illiteracy, the Central Zakat Committee, in October 1983, authorized local zakat committees to spend up to Rs. 100 ($8) per month to hire a secretary to read and keep records, and to prepare reports.

When asked why they serve on zakat committees, most members responded that they consider it an honor. Some consider it a religious obligation. It appears that some serve out of a sense of inherited responsibility: their families are relatively rich and have always been involved in whatever zakat activity was occurring. Most committees contain at least one mullah; often, local committees contain someone who has completed the *hajj* (pilgrimage to Mecca and Medina).

Local zakat committees are supposed to meet monthly, but according to their own reports, only about one-third actually do. Some meet bimonthly, others quarterly. About one-fourth meet only after they have received zakat funds in their local account; this occurs no more than twice a year, and maybe as infrequently as once every seven or eight months.

The biggest organizational problem facing local zakat committees is a result of their dependence on volunteers. Most local zakat committee members are elected because they are the leading men in a village. The same involvements which gain them respect take time in themselves and decrease the amount of time and energy these men can devote to zakat work. In some places, as members drift away or cease to be involved, no one remains to carry out the work of the committee and it ceases to function. Sometimes it is difficult for district and provincial zakat organizations to monitor the actual workings of the local committees. When questionnaires were sent to 5,000 chairmen of local zakat committees using the official roster of the Central Zakat Administration, about 10 percent were returned as undeliverable. Most of these committees had ceased to function, and no replacement committees had yet formed.

For all the emphasis on following the zakat format of the Qur'an, there is no precedent within Islamic shari'a for zakat disbursement or collection by committee. During the life of the Prophet, zakat was collected and disbursed by agents appointed by the Prophet, accountable to him, and paid from zakat funds. In Pakistan, an earlier official attempt in 1954 to establish zakat used the post office, not committees. The committee concept, unique to Pakistan, seems to have been a part of the discussion of a zakat system from at least 1978. Many interviewees speculated that the concept came from the widely established practice of having committees of locally selected volunteers manage the affairs of the local mosque. No one could recall, however, who actually posed the idea of committees, or when.

A few paid staff provide the skeletal framework supporting the zakat organization. The Administrator General Zakat, the Chief Administrators Zakat, and their subordinates are long-term professional civil servants. Whatever problems the government of Pakistan may have elsewhere with corruption, zakat officials not only function in a straightforward fashion, but go to some lengths to ensure that their activities remain respectable.

Below the provincial level, there is often no dedicated full-time staff assigned to zakat. At the district level, the deputy commissioner assigns what resources he can spare. Initially, the deputy commissioner was to be a member of the lcoal committee, but often didn't attend meetings. This was changed so that the deputy commissioner became the vice-chairman of the district zakat committee; following this change, attendance at meetings both by deputy commissioners and support personnel increased.

Completely outside the administrative structure of zakat is the National Zakat Foundation. Its name is a misnomer since it doesn't use zakat monies but is instead funded by an annual appropriation from the consolidated funds (i.e., general revenue), and makes grants to institutions serving mustahaqeen. These grants cover types of expenses proscribed by Hanafi tamlik, the requirement that zakat be given to a single donee. They are usually applied to the cost of buildings, equipment, and materials used in common by several mustahaqeen. Most grants given out to date by the National Zakat Foundation have provided start-up money for training centers or programs for women, the disabled, and orphans.

ELIGIBILITY DETERMINATION

The Zakat and 'Ushr Ordinance set broad parameters for eligibility for zakat, which is determined by local zakat committees. Priority is to be given to widows, orphans, the disabled, and students of *deeni madrasas* (traditional religious schools whose students have traditionally received zakat from private donors). If there is sufficient money, zakat funds may also be used for any of the eight types of poor specified in the shari'a, with the clear understanding that the committee is accountable to the authorities for money expended. Individuals who are denied zakat have the right to appeal the decision to the tehsil zakat committee.

These parameters give broad discretionary power to the local zakat committee. For administrative purposes, a person is eligible for zakat if the local committee says so, unless and until it can be demonstrated that he or she cannot be included under any of the eight categories specified by the shari'a. The only practical way to determine that someone is clearly not eligible is to prove that the person is a sahib-e-nisab (someone with more than enough wealth to meet his or her needs).

The largest single restraint on the local zakat committees' decisions is the very limited amount of money available for distribution. Ninety-five percent of the local zakat committees that were visited or that responded to the questionnaire said their largest problem was a lack of sufficient funds to meet the needs of everyone determined eligible.

Most committees depend on mustahaqeen to identify themselves and request zakat. Some committees use written application forms but most do not, since almost all the mustahaqeen are illiterate. In most instances, verification of eligibility is procured through a home visit by a member of the local zakat committee, in which the mustahaq is interviewed in private, sometimes along with neighbors.

Committees vary on the degree to which they prioritize. Some clearly attempt to provide regular modest funds to the most needy. Other committees say they try to give a little something to everyone.

The basic eligibility policy is very broad and flexible. It places a great deal of trust in the integrity, fairness, and good sense of the local zakat committee, holding them responsible for knowing their areas and for making sound and appropriate decisions.

The policy allows local zakat committees to be highly sensitive to individual problems and responsive to local priorities and needs. However, it also contains the potential for arbitrary and prejudiced decisions by local zakat committees. This is minimized by the fact that all seven members of a local zakat committee must reach a consensus before funds are distributed to a mustahaq. The community can exert social pressure on the committee if a decision is perceived as unfair. In rare instances, a case will be appealed to the tehsil zakat council, where the judgment of the chairman of the local zakat committee is scrutinized by the other local zakat committee chairmen in the tehsil.

In my visits to local committees, I observed that occasional complaints about eligibility were followed up. Usually, the person who complained about not receiving zakat was technically eligible, but had been passed over when local committee funds were insufficient to give zakat to all potentially eligible recipients. It was usually a judgment call as to which of the eligible people should receive a grant. Understandably, some of those technically eligible who didn't receive grants were upset by the decision.

DISBURSEMENT OF GRANTS

The amount of money disbursed as zakat grants varies widely, as does the frequency at which grants are distributed. Of the local zakat committees whose books I personally reviewed, grant amounts for a single person varied from a low of Rs. 12 ($1) per month in the Northwest Frontier Province, to a high of Rs. 400 ($30) per month in a section of Karachi. Returned surveys from 200 local zakat committees throughout Pakistan indicate that the great majority of zakat payments range from Rs. 50–100 per month for an individual, and Rs. 100–150 per month for a family.

When zakat first began, the maximum payment was set at Rs. 40 ($3) per month. Athar Mahmud of the Central Zakat Administration explains that the Central Zakat Committee realized this was inadequate to live on, but set the maximum benefit at that level because of its uncertainty about how much money would be collected and how many mustahaqeen there would be. Later, the Central Zakat Committee removed the upper limit.

Almost no one connected with the zakat system feels that zakat payments are adequate to live on. There was significant consensus among people interviewed (about 80 percent) that the absolute minimum subsistence level is Rs. 300 ($22) for an individual and Rs. 500–1,000 ($37–74) for a family. Clearly, most mustahaqeen do not receive this much. As a point of reference, Afghan refugees generally receive food, clothing, water, medical care, tents, blankets, and kerosene plus Rs. 150 ($11) a month each. Still another point of comparison is that the lowest federal monthly salary grade for a peon is Rs. 550 ($41).

The general expectation is that mustahaqeen will supplement their zakat benefits, although how they are expected to do this is not clear. This situation is problematic. Working at all may raise the expectation that they really are able to support themselves. However, many are too old or sick to work much even when work is available. They aren't supposed to beg, and if they do the local zakat committee may drop them. Most seem to eke out an existence on the generosity of neighbors, who give food, a little work, and a meager subsistence.

At this time, zakat is not adequate in the sense of fulfilling even the subsistence needs of people who cannot work to support themselves. It certainly is not a social security system (there is a limited system operating in Pakistan) ensuring a moderate level of comfort in the event of the injury or death of the primary earner. Yet before the zakat system was initiated, most of these mustahaqeen received far less than they receive now.

One of zakat's goals is to rehabilitate mustahaqeen to make them self-supporting. The most common form of "rehabilitation" practiced by about 80 to 90 percent of local zakat committees is to buy a mustahaq (usually a woman) a sewing machine. Most local committees simply provide the machine—no materials, thread, or scissors. Most important, most of these recipients are given no technical training nor are they taught how to establish and run a small business. Moreover, there is a limit to the number of people in a small village who can earn their living sewing, even if they are able to master the craft.

A few places have established training centers. Salai Markaz in Islamabad provides three to six months of training. While learning to sew in the program, women receive a training stipend, and are presented with a sewing machine at graduation. Even then, officials at Salai Markaz say that only some 10 to 15 percent of their graduates can actually support themselves.

Social welfare institutions for orphans and for the physically and mentally handicapped have benefitted greatly from zakat, as they now receive fairly generous grants for each recipient from provincial zakat administrations. For example, the Leprosy Hospital in Rawalpindi receives Rs. 500 per month for each patient.

Since its inception, the zakat system had disbursed more than Rs. 2,500 million to more than 4 million people by 1983 (Zia ul-Haq 1983: 16–18). While this has helped many individuals, the wide variance in payment levels and frequency of payments means that there is little equity in the program. The low levels of payment result in grants that are helpful, perhaps, but inadequate to fully support recipients living at subsistence levels.

IMPACT OF THE ZAKAT PROGRAM

The general public expectation—or at least hope—is that zakat will have an impact in one of four ways: 1) The provision of financial assistance to those who cannot work; 2) The economic rehabilitation of those who may be able to work to support themselves; 3) The elimination of beggary; 4) The redistribution of wealth in the society.

To date, most of the organizational effort of zakat has focused on the first goal. In various interviews conducted with recipients of zakat funds, when asked about the impact of zakat on their lives, most mustahaqeen said that they now eat a greater quantity and variety of food. For the most part, though, the amount of the grant has not been enough to make a substantive difference in lifestyle.

In economic rehabilitation, local zakat committees have been most successful with disabled men. Most of these men had worked and been exposed to the marketplace before becoming disabled. Zakat rehabilitation money has enabled them to buy a cart or a set of tools, or establish a shop. However, many local zakat committees have policies which inhibit individual initiative and strike particularly at the differences in the ways men and women are socialized. A number of local zakat committees stipulate that if an individual accepts a rehabilitation grant, he or she may never receive zakat again. This makes acceptance of a rehabilitation grant a statement of faith in one's ability to be self-supporting and a statement of acceptance of the role of wage-earner. Pakistani men are taught that to support themselves and their families is an integral part of their role. To a man, an opportunity to become self-supporting is an opportunity to regain an acceptable male role in society. Women, however, see their responsibilities as bearing, raising, and protecting their children; it is the responsibility of their male relatives to provide support. The acceptance of a rehabilitation grant aimed at making them self-supporting requires them to assume a nontraditional role for which they are usually unprepared.

One area in which zakat has made a difference is that of schooling. By paying school fees for many poor students, zakat has enabled them to attend school regularly, a modest but important effect.

The goal of eliminating beggary is problematic. Beggars make people feel uncomfortable, especially wealthy people. Many beggars are genuinely poor. Almost all are conspicuously crippled, maimed, or blind. For many of these people, begging is a profession by which they earn a living and support their families. Most beggars in Pakistan, especially in large cities, are part of large-scale organizations. Children are sometimes kidnapped, crippled, and then forced to beg. Zakat has little potential impact on what is essentially a law enforcement problem. Laws already in place give authorities the vehicle to eliminate beggary, but they are rarely enforced. Because of zakat, the public now has more insistant expectations that police will not allow beggars to beseech alms. Although the police have reduced the number of beggars on the streets, they have done this by intimidation and arrest, not by putting the beggars on zakat or offering them some other form of employment or welfare assistance.

For many Muslims, the ultimate goal of zakat is the elimination of poverty and of the extreme disparities of wealth existent in Pakistan: that is, income redistribution. However, for all practical purposes, no substantive redistribution has occurred. Zakat has had little secondary impact on the micro-economics of the village. On a larger scale, the recent macroeconomic model of Pakistan's economy (Naqvi 1983) contains no references to zakat. Naqvi considers zakat as too marginal to the economy to be considered a measurable factor. It must be combined with other elements of an Islamic economic system, for example, the elimination of *riba* (usury) and redistribution of lands to limits specified in the shari'a if economic redistribution is to occur.

The problem with making any impact by providing financial assistance to those who can't work is one of too many mustahaqeen and too little money. Money spent on maintenance has no dramatic "payoff." It has been a source of some frustration to the Central Zakat Committee and the Central Zakat Administration that as of January 1984, about 90 percent of the zakat funds expended had been disbursed to individual mustahaqeen for maintenance rather than for rehabilitation. At the same time, the very small size of zakat's grants means that zakat has no meaningful impact as a social security system or "safety net." Middle class and rich Muslims must pay zakat, but they cannot have any real expectation that they or their families will ever receive anything back from the system.

CONCLUSION

Viewed as a public welfare system, Pakistan's zakat program has been modestly successful. It has helped some people achieve financial independence, provided some income to help the poorest citizens survive, and enabled social welfare institutions to expand the quality of their programs and the number of people they can serve. Zakat has established a nationwide infrastructure blending volunteer committees and professional civil servants, mobilizing over a quarter-million members of the general population and involving them directly in zakat's implementation. The zakat system has promulgated eligibility criteria based on the Qur'an and shari'a that most people accept as reasonable and fair; these criteria are also flexible enough to allow local committees to interpret them in the light of local conditions. Zakat collection has demonstrated that the government can collect a tax impartially and efficiently, without corruption. Judged in terms of its help to the poor, the number of persons served, the amount of money collected and disbursed, and the equity of its benefits, Pakistan's zakat is a tremendous improvement over no government system at all.

However, although the zakat system has made a substantial beginning, it still has many limitations. The program is seriously underfunded to achieve even the most modest interpretation of its goals. Local committees express frustration over having insufficient funds to meet enormous need. Some committees fritter away what funds are available by giving grants so small they provide only marginal help. Except for a very few excellent training centers, most money spent on "rehabilitation" has shown little imagination or understanding of the spectrum of skills needed to operate a small business. Almost all local zakat committees are composed of men, who may not be sensitive to the needs of widows, the largest single group of mustahaqeen. The effectiveness of the aid given by local committees to mustahaqeen varies tremendously, depending on each committee's interest, commitment, and available time. Many members of the general public who approve of the basic concept of zakat question what real impact the system has had.

The biggest threat facing the success of the zakat system is that the same Islamization process which brought it into being seems to be fostering unreasonable and unrealistic expectations about what it—or any other welfare system—can do. Most of the general public, and many inside the system itself, do not recognize the inherent limitations of any welfare program working as a residual system, limited to responding to the immediate needs of individual persons. Zakat is not a development program. Those who expect it to eliminate poverty simply do not understand the dimensions and capabilities of a public welfare system, which cannot deal with the causes of poverty. Because of the enormity of Pakistan's widespread poverty and the limited funds actually available through zakat, the visible impact of the program is minimal. This, combined with high expectations, threatens the credibility of the system and could destroy it. In addition, the zakat system is threatened by the emotional and political baggage brought to it by many people, whose reaction to it is intertwined with their feelings about the nonelected government which imposed it.

All of these systemic problems, however, can be rationally dealt with to produce a more viable welfare system, as long as realistic expectations are set for it. If the zakat system can separate itself from national politics, rampant rhetoric, and Islamic fantasy, and concentrate on doing well the things that this system can do, it could be a very positive, if modest force, doing a lot of good for many people who need help. Pakistan has demonstrated by its initial achievements that the more modest goal is possible. However, if zakat alone is expected to eliminate all poverty and beggary, without other structural changes in the society, it will surely fail, and the opportunity to explore the potential for zakat as a welfare system in a modern state will be lost.

REFERENCES

Aghnides, Nicholas P. 1981. *An Introduction to Mohammedan Law.* Lahore: Sang-e-Meel Publications.

Ahmad, Khurshid. 1983. "Economic Development in an Islamic Framework." In *Studies in Islamic Economics.* Jeddah: The International Center for Research in Islamic Economics.

Ahmad, Shaikh Mahmud. 1952. *Economics of Islam.* 2nd ed. Lahore: Sheikh Muhammad Ashraf.

Flora, Peter and Arnold J. Heidenheimer, eds. 1981. *The Development of the Welfare State in Europe and America.* New Brunswick, N.J.: Transaction Books.

Government of Pakistan. 1980. *An Agenda for Islamic Economic Reforms: The Report of the Committee on Islamization Appointed by the Finance Minister.* Islamabad: Pakistan Institute of Development Economics.

Government of Pakistan, Ministry of Finance, Central Zakat Administration. 1982. *A Brief Introduction to the Zakat and 'Ushr System in Pakistan.* Islamabad: Government Printing Office.

Government of Pakistan, Ministry of Finance. 1980 *Report of the Committee on Islamization.* Islamabad: Pakistan Institute of Development Economics.

———. 1983. *Economic Survey of Pakistan, 1982–83*. Islamabad: Government Printing Office.
Haddad, Yvonne V. 1982. "The Islamic Alternative." *The Link* 15, No. 4 (September/October).
Maududi, Syed Abdul a'la. 1980. *Fundamentals of Islam*. Lahore: Islamic Publications.
Naqvi, Syed Nawab Haider. 1983. *Individual Freedom, Social Welfare and Islamic Economic Order.* Islamabad: Pakistan Institute of Development Economics.
Pusic, Eugene. 1971. *Social Welfare and Social Development*. The Hague: Mouton.
al-Qardawi, Allama Yusuf. 1981. *Economic Security in Islam*. Translated by Muhammad Iqbal Siddiqi. Lahore: Kazi Publications.
Qureshi, Anwar Iqbal. 1979. *The Economic and Social System of Islam*. Lahore: Islamic Book Service.
Sabzwari, M. A. 1979. *A Study of Zakat and 'Ushr with Special Reference to Pakistan*. Karachi: Industries Printing Press.
Sharif, M. Raihan. 1979. *Islamic Social Framework*. Lahore: Sheikh Muhammad Ashraf.
Siddiqi, Mohammad Akhfar Saeed. 1983. *Early Development of Zakat Law and Ijtihad*. Karachi: Islamic Research Academy.
Tanzil-ur-Rahman. 1981. *Introduction of Zakat in Pakistan*. Islamabad: Council of Islamic Ideology.
Wilensky, Harold L. and Charles V. Lebeaux. 1965. *Industrial Society and Social Welfare*. New York: The Free Press.
Zia ul-Haq, Mohammad. 1979. "Introduction of Islamic Laws: Address to the Nation." Islamabad, 10 February.
———. 1982. Interview at Rawalpindi, August 6.
———. 1983. "Constitutional Framework: Address to Majlis-e-Shoora," Islamabad, 12 August 1982. Interview at Rawalpindi, August 6.

6

Implications of the Islamization Program for Women

Anita M. Weiss

The current Islamization program has far-reaching implications for women in Pakistani society.[1] Supporters of Islamization assert that women will finally receive their due under Islamic law: that they will inherit lands; be protected by separate courts; and no longer face the indignity of laboring before men. Opponents contest this view, claiming that women are being demoted to second-class citizenship: that the meager social advances women enjoyed during the 1970s will disappear; their poverty will increase; their access to adequate health care and education will decrease; and their power, through participation in established social institutions—legal, educational, and political—will be systematically reduced. In an attempt to understand the foundations of both of these views, this chapter addresses the many implications of the new Islamic laws (both decreed and proposed) for women in Pakistan, discusses the variety of responses to these laws, and analyzes their effects on the social environment they are attempting to shape, focusing on the conflicting social forces at play.

Female literacy was at its peak in Pakistan in the mid-1970s, and women were just beginning to participate in larger numbers in both general elections and labor politics. The 1977 military coup d'état led by General Zia ul-Haq overthrew the government of former Prime Minister Zulfikar Ali Bhutto and effectively silenced political opposition for six years. Women protesting in demonstrations in Lahore and Karachi during February 1983 finally broke through the veil of silence which had fallen over Pakistan since Bhutto's execution. Prominent women—female lawyers and others—protesting the proposed Law of Evidence (viewed by many as subverting and limiting the position of women in Pakistan), suddenly changed the political realities in a country where the military had been seen as all-powerful. There is an apparent contradiction in policy as well as in thought regarding women's ideal and objective role: women's status has been simultaneously uplifted by the establishment of the women's Division in 1980—designed as part of the Cabinet Secretariat to safeguard and advance the position of women in the country—and diminished by the incorporation of certain Islamic laws, particularly the newly-decreed *Qanoon-e-Shahadat*, the Islamic Law of Evidence.

THE POSITION OF WOMEN IN PAKISTANI SOCIETY PRIOR TO THE ISLAMIZATION PROGRAM

Contradictions inherent within Islamic law also extend to women's position in society. This is evident in two of the strongest symbols of Islam: the Qur'an, which advocates the improvement of women's position and was a radical document for its time; and the veil, which physically limits women's participation in the larger society, effectively symbolizing her powerlessness.

The legal position of Muslim women is guaranteed in the Qur'an which acknowledges such practices as female inheritance (albeit at half the share that a man inherits), female consent to marriage, and remarriage by widows and divorcees. However, Muslim women's options have traditionally been limited in northern India more by customs and attitudes than by religious law, so that these legal rights have not always been exercised. In addition, whereas Islam encourages a woman to be literate so she can read from the Qur'an and educate her children, the gender discrimination in Pakistan becomes apparent when we realize that barely one-sixth of the female population has had a minimum schooling of three years. According to official estimates, only 13 percent of all females in Pakistan can "read a newspaper and write a letter," giving Pakistan one of the lowest female literacy levels in the world.[2]

The most obvious restriction on women stems from the institution of *purdah*, the formalized separation of women from the world of men. Though purdah literally means "curtain" in Urdu, it has come to connote both the physical and practical separations between the activities of men and women (Papanek 1973). Although not all women observe the restrictions it imposes, most do embrace the inherent values, for example, that a woman preserves her family's *izzat* (honor) by not mixing with unrelated men and by not wearing revealing clothes. A woman who does these things acts outside the traditional parameters of respectability.

Purdah has been an issue only for the wealthier classes, however. Poorer woman, who have had to work for subsistence, have never had the leisure to observe purdah or to wear the veil. Even among wealthier women, many in metropolitan areas such as Karachi, Lahore, and Islamabad no longer strictly adhere to traditional modest dress; the *dupatta*, for example, is often used in such cities as a colorful accessory rather than as a functional piece of clothing.[3]

Between Independence in 1947 and 1979, only two substantial legal reforms affected women's position in Pakistan. In 1961, the Ayub Khan government introduced the Muslim Family Laws Ordinance, which reformed the Muslim Personal Law (Shariat) Application Act of 1937. This progressive document ensured women's rights in divorce, inheritance by grandchildren, and the written consent of a man's first wife before he could marry a second one.[4] Later, the 1973 Constitution advanced women's position by prohibiting discrimination on the basis of sex. Despite the Bhutto government's slogan of "Islamic Socialism," however, no other legal changes specifically addressed the position of women.

LEGAL EFFECTS, BOTH DECREED AND PROPOSED

The introduction of Islamic economic measures has had minimal impact on women, since few women work to earn cash (they instead work for subsistence) and those who do rarely enjoy enough surplus to pay an alms tax or open a savings account.[5] Instead, women are often recipients of the zakat funds. General Zia ul-Haq (1983:16–18) reported that Rs. 2,550 million has been distributed among widows, orphans, and the needy since the beginning of the zakat program.

Judicial reforms include the incorporation of a Federal Shariat Court and the appointment of religious scholars as *qazis* (judges) to the Supreme Court. Initially, conservatives argued that a woman should not serve as a qazi under Islam. Then in August 1982, in a case brought before the Federal Shariat Court, the attorney general quoted shari'a sources and proved that there was no ban on women functioning as qazis. Military courts, however, could overrule decisions taken by the Shariat and civil courts; the latter may not contest the military courts' actions. In December

1983, General Zia announced that in order for Pakistan to progress, due rights and status must be given to women, and that they must not be confined to *chador aur char diwari* (the veil and the four walls of the home). To give women the power to secure their rights and status under Islam, it was decided that separate courts, employing female staff, would be set up to deal with cases involving women.[6] However, as of this writing, this decision has not yet been implemented.

Along with its judicial reforms, Pakistan established a consultative federal assembly, the Majlis-e-Shura. No gender restrictions were placed on membership. The assembly was set up to offer advice and debate issues, and federal elections for it were held in February 1985. Of the eleven female candidates—seven from Punjab and two each from Sind and the Northwest Frontier Province—only one woman, Syeda Abida Hussain from District Jhang in Punjab, was elected.[7]

In implementing an Islamic penal code, Pakistan established hudud punishments for the crimes of burglary, murder, intoxication, adultery, and perjury. Under this system, women are most affected by the promulgation of the Offense of Zina (adultery) Act. The legal definition of *zina* follows: "a [sane] adult man and a [sane] adult woman are said to commit 'zina' if they wilfully have sexual intercourse without being validly married to each other" (Ordinance No. 7 of 1979, Part 4).

Another part of the ordinance addresses *zina-bil-jabr*, which consists of four types of sexual intercourse without consent, that is, rape. General Zia ul-Haq (1979:19) has pronounced that a person may be proven guilty of zina-bil-jabr "with or without the consent of the parties." However, evidence for zina-bil-jabr remains the same as for any other hadd crime: the severest punishment (death by stoning or one hundred lashes) is invoked only if the evidence includes either the accused's confession or the testimony of four salah (morally upright) adult Muslim males. Without such evidence, the penalty is at the court's discretion.

However, such punishments have been meted out in a highly discriminatory fashion. Women have been proven guilty of zina-bil-jabr through medical examinations following the rape, or because they became pregnant and were unmarried. The best-known case is that of Safia Bibi, a young blind woman who had been hired as a domestic servant and became pregnant following a multiple rape. She was given a punishment of fifteen lashes for zina-bil-jabr. The two men involved—a father and his son—were not punished: the former was not charged because of lack of evidence and the latter was acquitted by being given the "benefit of the doubt." Heated disputes have erupted regarding this policy. Besides the issue of whether a woman should suffer twice, many consider that this law discriminates against women by accepting illegitimate birth as a form of "confession" proving a woman's guilt while the man goes unpunished.[8] Yet it is nearly impossible to prove a man's guilt without his verbal confession, for what four salah Muslim men would stand by and let a woman be raped? In August 1983, the Federal Shariat Court did reverse the ruling of the session judge in this case and distinguished between rape and adultery, dismissing Safia Bibi's sentence. Lal Mai, a thirty-five-year-old woman from Liaqatpur (Bahawalpur district), was not as lucky; on 30 September 1983, she became the first woman to be publicly whipped for adultery under the new laws. Eight thousand people are said to have watched her receive fifteen lashes. A woman in Swat was later sentenced to receive eighty lashes. The men in both cases were acquitted. The Women's Action Forum and the Pakistan Women Lawyers Association have protested the floggings as "degrading, unnecessary, brutal, and a direct violation of the International Declaration of Human Rights, to which Pakistan is a signatory."[9]

A recent case heard before the Federal Shariat Court involved a husband and wife who had been arrested under Sections 10 and 11 of the hudud ordinance because a baby girl was born to them only seven and a half months after their marriage. They were initially sentenced to three years' rigorous imprisonment, thirty lashes, and a fine of Rs. 1,000 each for having had illicit sexual relations before the date of their *Nikah* (Muslim marriage ceremony). However, the Federal Shariat Court acquitted them upon appeal.[10]

The fiat potentially most damaging to women's equity is the newly-pronounced Qanoon-e-Shahadat (Law of Evidence), recommended by the advisory Council on Islamic Ideology to the president in late January 1983. The Ordinance modifies the Evidence Law enacted during the British Raj in 1940. The Majlis-e-Shura approved it in February 1983, except for one controversial clause. Two versions of the clause were under discussion: the first would allow evidence by two witnesses in most instances (except where other requirements were invoked); the second would necessitate evidence by "two Muslims and in the absence of two male witnesses by the evidence of one male and two female witnesses." The clause finally included reads: "The number and particulars of the witnesses would be in accordance with the Holy Qur'an and Sunnah, the details of which are as under: in Hudud, according to the Hudud Ordinance. In Qisas, according to the Qisas and Diyat ordinances. In other matters, two men or one man and two women. If the said witnesses are not available, the court shall decide on the evidence of one woman or such other evidence and circumstances as may be available."[11] According to this interpretation, women would be prohibited from testifying in a hadd case.

After its passage in the Majlis-e-Shura and its recommendation to the president, demonstrations protesting the ordinance broke out in Lahore and Karachi, jointly led by women of varying political and social backgrounds. When police lathi-charged some of the female demonstrators in Lahore on 12 February 1983, the assault on the women was also denounced by politically diverse groups. A number of arguments were presented showing that the proposed Law of Evidence was not the only acceptable evidence law in Islam. Members of the Women's Action Forum and the Pakistan Women Lawyers Association contested that there is only one instance in the Qur'an, Ayat 282 (Sura al-Baqr), in which two women are called to testify in the place of one man. This, however, is in a specific financial arrangement, and the role of the second woman is to remind the first on points which she may have forgotten. In numerous other ayats, men and women are referred to as being equal in matters of witness.[12] Critics also note that the testimony of Hazrat Khadija, the Prophet's first wife, asserting that Muhammad was the Prophet of God, made her the Prophet's first disciple. On the single testimony of Hazrat Aisha (another of the Prophet's wives), hundreds of hadith have been verified. In addition, a rigid interpretation of the Qur'an, such as would support the Law of Evidence (i.e., meaning "male" whenever the generic word "man" was used) would virtually exclude women from being members of the religion.

Concerning the exclusion of women's evidence as inadmissible in hudud cases, it has been charged that the sole evidence of Hazrat Naila, the wife of Usman (the third Caliph), was accepted by the Prophet's companions as proof of the guilt of Usman's murderer. Opponents of the Law of Evidence argue that the criteria for witnesses as stated in the Qur'an are possession of sight, memory, and the ability to communicate. As long as witnesses have these—be they men or women—their testimony should be admissible.

The interpretation finally decreed into law in October 1984 restricts the testimony of two women being equal to that of one man only to financial cases; otherwise, it is left up to the discretion of the judge.[13]

Another law proposed by the Council on Islamic Ideology but not yet decreed is the Law of Qisas (retaliation) and Diyat (blood money). If a man is murdered, the law allows for a diyat equivalent to 30.4 kilos of silver; if a woman is murdered, the diyat is to be only half of that. If a woman is physically harmed, the compensation is again only half that which would be given to a man.[14] Critics claim that it is illogical for the punishment for murder to be equal for men and women (death for both) while the diyat differs depending on whether the murder victim is a man or a woman.[15]

The Ansari Commission was assembled in 1982 with the purpose of informing the president as to which aspects of contemporary society were repugnant to Islam. It has since recommended a number of controversial measures. These include disqualifying women from ever being the head of state; requiring a woman to be at least fifty years of age (a man need be only twenty-five) and to secure her husband's permission before becoming a member of the Majlis-e-Shura; guaranteeing that 5 percent of the general membership of the Majlis-e-Shura for the next ten years be reserved for women (to be appointed by the president); prohibiting women from leaving the country without a male escort; and refusing to allow an unmarried, unaccompanied woman to serve abroad in the foreign service.

The above three sets of proposals—the Law of Evidence, the Law of Qisas and Diyat, and the Ansari Commission's measures—have all met with substantial resistence from educated women throughout Pakistan. Cries of discrimination against women were raised as concern mounted that women were officially being relegated to second-class status. Syeda Abida Hussain, Chairman of the Jhang District Council and the sole female member of the Majlis-e-Shura, has said that women in Pakistan are now in the midst of fighting the biggest *jihad* (holy war) in history, and that "Islam enjoins rights and responsibilities on Muslim women which are not subject to any dispute."[16]

The Women's Action Forum, composed of female lawyers and other concerned women, has taken an active stand against these three proposals. Other women are studying Islamic laws and their application to women throughout the Muslim world. Begum Ra'ana Liaquat Ali Khan, President of the All-Pakistan Women's Association, has also taken a strong stand against the proposals' promulgation. She asserts that "some clauses about women in the Ansari Commission Report are repugnant to the Holy Qur'an and Islam, which gives women equal rights with men in all public matters."[17]

Other critics of the Ansari Commission Report have noted that there have been women rulers in Muslim history, such as Bilquis, Queen of Sheba, and two queens in Yemen during the Sulaihid dynasty.[18] They have also used the example of Miss Fatima Jinnah, the sister of the Quaid-e-azam, who ran for the office of president against Ayub Khan in 1963.

In November 1985, the International Women Lawyers Conference convened in Lahore and, led by the Pakistan Women Lawyers Association, urged the Pakistan government to sign the United Nations Convention on the Elimination of Discrimination against Women, and to support the establishment of a "nongovernment international commission. . . . to recommend a uniform and universal code of personal laws under Islam with equal representation of women and embodying these in specific provisions of law in the light of international norms and standards of justice, peace and equity."[19]

Not all segments of the society reject Pakistan's conservative proposals, however. The Majlis-e-Khawatin-i-Pakistan, another women's group, rejects the validity of the United Nations Convention on the Elimination of Discrimination against Women by claiming it is repugnant to Islam. This group also supported the police lathi-charge of the protesting women in Lahore and Karachi. The Jama'at-i-Tulaba, a student group affiliated with the Jama'at-i-Islami, which has long supported the conservative policies of the government (including the dismissal of left-oriented faculty members from the universities and the division of educational institutions by sex), has also opposed the Women's Action Forum on these issues. Responding to the argument against the proposed Qanoon-e-Shahadat, that it is based on only one Qur'anic ayat, some 'ulema have asserted that "disagreement with any verse of the Holy Qur'an is tantamount to rejecting the whole of [the] Qur'an."[20]

Besides making legal changes, the government has supported its Islamization program through a number of directives and official positions. In terms of women's work options, thus far the effects of such directives have been minimal. Social values often constrain women from wanting to mix with men at the workplace while economic and political priorities tend to make unions exclude women from membership in their ranks.[21]

The effects of Islamization at the workplace are largely cosmetic: employers set aside an area of the factory for prayers or women are advised to dress modestly, often even to wear their dupattas on their heads. Female newscasters on television have had to cover their heads since 1979. No mention, however, is made of proper attire for men, who by any strict interpretation of the Qur'an should also wear loose, unrevealing clothes, and most certainly not tight blue jeans. When the question of proper dress for men is ignored, the emphasis placed on it for women can only be regarded as discriminatory.

The new educational policy has had important implications for women. Compulsory courses in Qur'anic studies and Islamiyat have been introduced throughout the educational system, and Urdu has become the official language of instruction. Textbooks have been revised to conform with Islamic teachings. An Islamic University has also been established.

The most important change for women has come via a presidential proposal planning the establishment of a women's university. This will consist of university colleges throughout the country. The home economics colleges at Karachi, Lahore, and Peshawar are slated to be upgraded and affiliated with the women's university. It is promised, though, that women will still have the option to seek admission to coeducational universities. Critics of the proposal claim that such a university will increase women's isolation, and this at the level of the brightest, most educated women. The women's university will stress home economics, medicine, and teaching, leaving women's education deficient in technology and the physical and social sciences.

ISLAMIZATION AND SOCIAL CHANGE FOR WOMEN

The government, in response to its critics, has maintained that it is simply trying to get rid of anti-Islamic elements in the society. It has claimed that, under its tutelage, the position of women has in fact improved. Mahbubul Haq, chairman of the Planning Commission responsible for the Sixth Five-Year Plan (1983–88) has said that Islam is a great liberator of both men and women, and should never be used for oppressing either, and that in fact a quiet revolution has been occurring in Pakistan over the past twenty years with increasing enrollment of females in primary schools, colleges, and universities as well as increasing numbers of women competing in the job market.[22] He emphasized that the government remains supportive of these goals.

The report of the Working Group on Women's Development Programmes for the Sixth Plan noted the problem of the invisibility of women workers in areas where they are in fact contributing to the country's economic development. The report recommended that Rs. 5 million (above that already being spent on ongoing projects) be used for development programs in education, culture, health, population welfare, agriculture, employment, industry, and mass communications with a focus on women. Although Mahbubul Haq at first publically agreed with the report, very limited resources have been set aside for women's projects.

The Women's Action Forum criticized the authors of the Sixth Plan for not providing adequate funds and for failing to recognize the contributions of women's work to the national economy. The planners had estimated that only .5 million women (out of a total 18.3 million women) in rural areas are economically active, and that there were only 176 females working in agriculture and animal husbandry. Any observer of Pakistan's society can easily conclude that women engaged in subsistence economies have been omitted from such analyses.

Pakistan faces many other social problems (including institutionalized gender inequality in access to health resources; an appallingly high population growth rate of 3 percent annually which causes the population to double every twenty-three years; and serious health problems—for example, 90 percent of all women suffer from some sort of anemia during their child-bearing years) and the role which Islam may play in alleviating these remains unclear. One Qur'anic injunction which has helped poor rural children in Pakistan refers to breast-feeding: boys are to be breast-fed until twenty-two months, girls until twenty-four months. In 1975, the Pakistan Fertility Survey (part of the World Fertility Survey) found that 99 percent of rural children were being breast-fed for long durations. Problems associated with infant formula diets are not as pervasive in Pakistan as in other Third World countries for this reason.

An Islamic perspective in the issue of family planning can be approached from two directions. Some claim that Islam supports family planning on the basis that it protects the health of the mother; others claim that Islam strictly forbids it. Pakistan does have a relatively successful family planning program in progress, ably headed by Dr. Attiya Inayatullah, who has been lauded by the United Nations for her past work. A resolution proposed at the November 1985 International Women Lawyers Conference in Lahore supporting women's right to abortion in Pakistan was not passed.

A final change brought about by Pakistan's Islamization efforts is one which cannot readily be observed, but can be discovered only through discussion. People, at least in urban areas, are now thinking about where Islam fits into their "secular" lives in an unprecedented way. Because of the government laws and directives, many people are discussing and trying to decipher what Islam does mean to them, and the extent to which they—on a personal level—wish to integrate Islamic teachings into their lives. The Women's Action Forum is holding Arabic classes to counter charges by fundamentalists that its members are a small minority of Westernized women who don't understand or care about Islam. Likewise, instead of responding to the assault on the women demonstrators in February 1983 by appealing to parliamentary law and civil rights doctrines, the Pakistan Women Lawyers Association brought suit against the government on Islamic legal grounds that the police, as unrelated men, had no right to touch the demonstrating women. Although women have not yet lost any rights, many of them are thinking about the implications of the proposals and taking an active stand one way or the other. While in the past, the All-Pakistan Women's Association was regarded as an organization made up of *begums* with time on their hands, its activist position against the proposed Qanoon-e-Shahadat and the Ansari Commission's Report is changing the way people think about it, and increasing its potential for facilitating real social change.

SOME REASONS BEHIND THE PROPOSALS ON WOMEN

Particular kinds of social relationships are encouraged by the types of existing laws in every society. Traditional Islamic law as applied in South-Asia has favored the maintenance of extended patrilineal kinship networks and the control of women through male members in these networks, primarily in a rural subsistence economy. Reforms occur generally because of changes in political and economic institutions. Anderson and Coulson (1983:86–87) write that it is "obvious that the future of Islamic law cannot be separated from the economic, political and social future of the countries in which it is applied." David Taylor (1983:182) believes that Pakistan's problems stem from trying to reconcile and integrate "a set of not always fully consistent ideological perspectives with the political legacies of the past and the constraints of the present." Therefore, to what can we attribute Pakistan's affirmation of Islamic law and integration of it into the government's legal apparatus and, in this instance, Pakistan's affirmation of a conservative interpretation of Hanafi fiqh?

Informal sanctions in Pakistan have historically played far more significant roles in restricting women's position than have the recent parcel of official directives, which have affected women in three major areas: education, legal participation, and punishments (especially regarding adultery).[23] For example, except under extreme duress, women would rarely testify in the courts anyhow. Few women care if a woman's university exists or not, for the majority are poor, illiterate rural inhabitants, eeking out a subsistence from the land supplemented by the remnants of traditional craftsmanship. Lucy Carroll (1982:66) argues that the present government is taking the constitutional mandate that all existing laws be brought into conformity with the injunctions of Islam much more seriously than have any of its predecessors. This is occurring despite the fact that the government has suspended the 1973 Constitution.

We must surmise that there are reasons motivating the government to enact these measures other than simple religious or parliamentary ones.

One possible reason is that the Islamization program is being used to placate the government's political supporters, particularly the Jama'at-i-Islami. By proposing laws based on religion yet not enforcing them, the government can appease the fundamentalists without challenging other powerful groups (consisting of men) within the society. So many other areas could have been focused on (e.g., redistribution of wealth, especially of rural land-holdings; establishment of an Islam-based political decision-making process; formation of social programs stressing man's obligations to God's creation, *haquq ul-abad*), that the fact that women have been singled out is significant. General Zia ul-Haq (1983:35–37) has said that the government's first priority is to "carry forward the process of Islamization and to consolidate the measures already taken in this behalf to a degree that no future Government can reverse them." But then he proceeds to mention goals similar to those of most developing Third World countries, concluding with a wish to accelerate the pace of development programs so that the "maximum possible area may be provided with the amenities of [the] modern age in the minimum possible time."

When General Zia announced, on 20 December 1983, that the Qanoon-e-Shahadat would be sent to the provincial governments before being sent for approval to the federal cabinet, sources in the Women's Division felt that it would never be passed into law, but that General Zia was using it to appeal to the fundamentalists. They still feel strongly that the Qisas and Diyat ordinances will not be decreed. Although many in the government do realize that the majority of female defendants in adultery/rape cases brought to court have been poor, rural women or members of destitute families unable to hire lawyers and without political influence, no one in power appears to recognize which segments of the female population are most affected by the new laws; in fact, they are upholding class distinctions as well as gender discrimination.

Another possible reason behind the government's proposals concerning women is that by enforcing traditional law, they are sustaining a certain type of economy. Social scientists generally agree that the secularization of society is an indicator of the transformation from feudal relations to capitalist ones. For example, in Tunisia, the Code of Personal Status (a reinterpretation of Islamic law giving women full rights and responsibilities in the society) affirms the nuclear family, which is fast becoming the more popular form. Mounira Charrad believes that the Tunisian state changed the law to break down the internal solidarity of kin groupings, which had already broken down enough to make this possible.[24] The movement towards the nuclear family, which strengthens the husband/wife relationship, and away from separatist kinship groupings, helps the development of secular, centralized institutions. Also, by making a woman responsible for the needs of her family (if she is in a position to be so), the Code of Personal Status in Tunisia not only affirms the nuclear family, but connotes the transformation of economic relations, that is, the capitalization of the economy, by including women and recognizing their economic importance. This is not being done in Pakistan, perhaps due to the as yet incomplete transition to a capitalist economy, which has made migrant laborers to the Gulf States Pakistan's greatest export and source of foreign exchange. In a system where few are benefitting from capitalist relations, it would be difficult for Pakistan to favor secular laws promoting them.

Finally, another factor contributing to the government's position on women is one which plagues most other governments and international organizations as well: there are few hard facts illuminating what women do. The dispute in Pakistan concerning the proper role for women extends virtually throughout the Third World. In the past, international development agencies such as UNDP, FAO, and US AID have done much to perpetuate the Western stereotype of women's position being in the home and nurturing her children. This role is in fact alien to most Third World women, including a majority of Pakistani women, who must toil in the fields or trade in the marketplace for their family's subsistence (Rogers 1980:79–120). Usually, only wealthier women have the leisure time to participate in the kinds of projects these agencies design, which ostensibly help poor women but actually serve only elites. The All-Pakistan Women's Association has also implemented such programs in Pakistan, establishing income-generating projects such as tablecloth-making, baking, and rug weaving without ensuring adequate local mass-marketing networks. Instead, the products were "oriented towards the limited and unreliable tourist and overseas specialty markets."[25] Yet people felt they were "doing something good for women."

The government's proposal for a separate women's university would merely perpetuate this lack of knowledge about women's needs. In rural areas, women who must forage for firewood, transport water from wells, transplant rice, and cut alfalfa for their animals, among other tasks, do not need lessons in home economics. Nor do they need to be told to wear their dupattas on top of their heads. They do need to be put into contact with new forms of technology that will help them survive, and to learn how to read so as to implement their newly learned skills, perhaps freeing up some time so they can send a child to school.

Social scientists have documented problems in projects such as family planning and health care when they are organized by men without the immediate input of women.[26] Such projects designed by men to control women's fertility are often doomed to failure, for the men are unaware of the women's primary concerns and fears. Likewise, a weakness can be seen in a process where men are adapting Islamic laws to women. At the least, women educated in the study of the Qur'an should be invited to offer suggestions. Instead, they have been excluded. The Special Committee on the Evidence Act of the Federal Shariat Court is made up of four men: three judges of the Supreme Court and Tanzil-ur-Rehman, chairman of the Council on Islamic Ideology. They are the ones who have decided that a woman's testimony should not be admissible in a court of law, are questioning if she can study with male students, and are even announcing how she should act to preserve her modesty. The lack of female input becomes evident when one reviews the contradictory proposals.

It is interesting that protests against the ordinances that would codify women's subordinate position cut across class lines. This is significant in Pakistan mostly because it is very rare. Yet it is characteristic of most viable women's movements throughout the world: the realization that women must band together to overcome social injustice and ensure a better future.

NOTES

1. An earlier version of this chapter appeared in *Asian Survey*, 25, No. 8 (August 1985:863–80).

2. The 1981 Government of Pakistan Census reports a 13.5 percent total female literacy rate: 33.7 percent for urban women; 5.5 percent for rural women. This is up from the 1972 statistics, which registered rates of 11.6 percent overall, 30.9 percent for urban women, and 4.7 percent for rural women.

3. The dupatta, essentially a diaphanous veil, serves a very important function in traditional society, as it assists women in covering both their hair and their "bodily ornaments." Thin skarves are now occasionally substituted for the dupatta in urban areas, making it merely a fashionable ornament.

4. My purpose here is not to elaborate on the various rights which women received under the 1961 law. For further information, see Carroll (1981). It has been shown that few women have benefited from the family laws pertaining to maintenance after divorce.

5. For information on women's increased participation in Pakistani polity and industry, consult Hafeez (1983) and Weiss (1984a).

6. *The Muslim*, 20 December 1983.

7. These figures are based on election results published in *Pakistan Affairs* 38, No. 5 (1 March 1985), which is an official publication of the Pakistan Embassy in Washington, D.C.

8. *Viewpoint* (15 July 1983) poignantly addresses the issue of flogging rape victims. Another case was reported in *The Muslim*, 21 February 1983.

9. *The Muslim*, 4 October 1983. Pakistan, however, is not a signatory of the United Nations Convention on the Elimination of Discrimination against Women.

10. This was reported in the daily newspaper *Dawn* on 4 November 1985. No reason was stated for the acquittal.

11. *Dawn* (5 March 1983), published this quote from the ordinance.

12. See for example sura Al-Noor, verses 6, 7, 8, and 9.

13. This analysis is based on conversations with Kemal Faruki, barrister at law, in December 1984.

14. *Dawn* (Supplement), December 1983.

15. William L. Richter (1985:150) reports that a later draft by the Majlis-e-Shura modifies the references to women.

16. *The Muslim*, 17 February 1983.

17. *Dawn*, 5 September 1983. See also *Dawn*, 9 September 1983 and *The Muslim*, 14 September 1983 on this issue.

18. For further information on women Muslim rulers, refer to Waddy (1980:91–98). See also Parveen Shaukat Ali, *Status of Women in the Muslim World* (Lahore, 1975).

19. *Dawn*, 7 November 1985.

20. *Dawn*, 18 February 1983.

21. In an earlier study of women working in the pharmaceutical industry in Lahore, women often told me that they preferred conditions (e.g., separate rooms in which to work) under which purdah could be observed. For further information, see Weiss (1984b).

22. *The Muslim*, 17 May 1983.

23. Michelle Maskiell addresses the issue of culture and tradition preventing women from participating fully in legal, educational, and other institutions in "The Effects of Islamization on Pakistani Women's Lives, 1978–1983," an unpublished paper presented at the South Asia Conference, Madison, Wisconsin, November 1983.

24. Mounira Charrad, professor of sociology at the University of California, San Diego, has written extensively on legal reforms and women's rights in North Africa. This information on the Personal Code in Tunisia was relayed through personal discussions.

25. Rogers (1980:95) reports that this fact haunts the marketing structure of women's projects throughout the Third world.

26. Pat Barnes-McConnell and Dora G. Lodwick discuss these kinds of problems at length in *Working with International Development Projects: A Guide for Women-in-Development* (East Lansing, Michigan: Office of Women in Development, Michigan State University, 1983).

REFERENCES

Anderson, Jerome D. and Norman J. Coulson. 1983. In *Islamic Law in Contemporary Cultural Change*, edited by M. Farani. Lahore: Lahore Law Times Publications.

Ayoob, Mohammed, ed. 1981. *The Politics of Islamic Reassertion*. London: Croom Helm Ltd.

Beck, Lois and Nikki Keddie, eds. 1978. *Women in the Muslim World*. Cambridge: Harvard University Press.

Carroll, Lucy. 1981. "Muslim Family Law in South Asia: Important Decisions Regarding Maintenance for Wives and Ex-wives." *Islamic and Comparative Law Quarterly* 1: 95–113.

———. 1982. "Nizam-i-Islam: Processes and Conflicts in Pakistan's Programme of Islamisation, with Special Reference to the Position of Women." *Journal of Commonwealth and Comparative Politics* 20: 57–95.

Esposito, John L. 1982. *Women in Muslim Family Law*. Syracuse: Syracuse University Press.

Government of Pakistan. 1979. *Islamic Laws (Enforcement of Nizam-E-Mustafa)*. Lahore: Lahore Law Times Publications.

———. 1982. *New Islamic Criminal Laws*. Lahore: Lahore Law Times Publications.

———. 1983. *Revival of Islamic Values*. Islamabad: Pakistan Publications.

Government of Pakistan, Ministry of Law and Parliamentary Affairs. 1980. *The Pakistan Penal Code, 1860 (As Modified up to 3rd February, 1980)*. Karachi: Manager of Publications.

Government of Pakistan, Women's Division. n.d. *Development Programmes and Projects for Women in Pakistan: July 1980 to June 1981*. Islamabad.

Hafeez, Sabeeha. 1983. *Women in Industry: Phase I, Basic Survey.* Report prepared under the auspices of the Women's Division, Cabinet Secretariat, Government of Pakistan. Islamabad.

Papanek, Hanna. 1973. "Purdah: Separate Worlds and Symbolic Shelter." *Comparative Studies on Society and History*, 15, No. 3: 289–325.

———. 1981. "The Differential Impact of Programs and Policies on Women in Development." In *Women and Technological Change in Developing Countries*, edited by Roslyn Dauber and Melina Cain. Boulder: Westview Press.

Patel, Rashida. 1979. *Women and Law in Pakistan*. Karachi.

Richter, William L. 1985. "Pakistan in 1984: Digging In." *Asian Survey*, 25, No. 2 (February): 145–54.

———. 1979. "The Political Dynamics of Islamic Resurgence in Pakistan." *Asian Survey*, 19, No. 6 (June): 547–57.

Rogers, Barbara. 1980. *The Domestication of Women: Discrimination in Developing Societies*. London: Tavistock Publications.

Smith, Jane. 1980. *Women in Contemporary Muslim Societies*. Lewisburg, Pa.: Bucknell University Press.

Tanzil-ur-Rehman. 1978. *Islamization of Pakistan Law*. Karachi: Hamdard Academy.

Taylor, David. 1983. "The Politics of Islam and Islamization in Pakistan." In *Islam in the Political Process*, edited by James P. Piscatori. Cambridge: Cambridge University Press.

Waddy, Charis. 1980. *Women in Muslim History*. London: Longman Group.

Weiss, Anita M. 1984a. "The Power of Tradition in the Modern Industrial Sector:

Female Factory Workers in Pakistan." Paper presented at the conference on Pakistan's Future Prospects, Columbia University, October.
———. 1984b. "Tradition and Modernity at the Workplace: A Field Study of Women in the Pharmaceutical Industry of Lahore." *Women's Studies International Forum* 7, No. 4:259–64.
Zafar, Emmanuel. 1981. *Law and Practice of Islamic Hudood*. Lahore: Khyber Law Publishers.
Zia ul-Haq, Mohammad. 1979. "Introduction of Islamic Laws: Address to the Nation." Islamabad, 10 February.
———. 1983. "Constitutional Framework: Address to Majlis-e-Shoora." Islamabad, 12 August.

Newspapers and Periodicals

Dawn. Karachi.
Far Eastern Economic Review. Hong Kong.
International Herald Tribune.
The Muslim. Rawalpindi.
Times of Pakistan. Islamabad.
Viewpoint. Lahore.

7

Islamization: A View from the Countryside

Richard Kurin

From reading the Pakistani newspapers, watching television, and listening to the pronouncements of government officials, particularly in the light of the December 1984 referendum, one gets the impression that Islamization is a major goal of Pakistani society[1] and that there is indeed a broad consensus concerning its relevance and desirability. Islamization is a popular topic in Pakistan—the subject of speeches, books, articles, conversations, and even programs in American Centers. Where it is found, critical analysis of the present government-sponsored Islamization program focuses on three central questions. First, how relevant is Islamization to various segments of Pakistani society, beyond those of officialdom and such organizations as the Jama'at-i-Islami? Second, what does Islamization mean and how is the issue of varying interpretations and modes of interpretation to be resolved? And finally, how should Islamization apply to specific issues and policies, such as national development, women's rights, and scientific education?

To be sure, there is considerable debate on each of these points. Polar positions are easily characterized. Some people are sure that everyone agrees with and enthusiastically supports Islamization, while others are equally certain that Islamization is a fraud, a tool used by a dictatorial regime to further its own ends. Some Pakistanis have argued that Islamization is self-evident and has a single meaning held by everyone in the Muslim community, while others counter that Islamization is a vague concept with different communities and sects holding different and often contradictory interpretations of what it entails. Some envision Islamization as changing the nature of Pakistani society, seeing it as the means of putting all women in purdah, promulgating religious modes of education, and strictly enforcing shariat law. For others, Islamization means expanding gender role equality, pursuing scientific knowledge, and applying traditional moral principles to contemporary circumstances.

While such differences abound, it is clear that Islamization, at least at the level of national discourse, is a core symbol for the presentation of products and issues. How else can one explain the current vogue of Islamic clothing, Islamic soft drinks, Islamic economics, Islamic medicine, Islamic television, Islamic sociology and anthropology, and that favorite, the Islamic bomb? Issues associated with the role of women, education, development, and national identity preceded the regime of Zia ul-Haq. Yet in current discourse such issues have been redefined and recontextualized, calling upon Islamic terms and concepts, Islamic sources and bases of legitimacy for their resolution.

But what about Islamization in rural areas, where the government is more distant, newspapers unread, and televisions few and far between? Is Islamization even relevant, let alone an idiom for debate? What does Islamization mean in the countryside? And to what issues is it applied there?

Pakistan's villages constitute the home of the vast majority of the country's population. And yet the voices of villagers either do not reach or are ignored by Pakistani elites and urban-centered foreign scholars. Government officials, the media, and Pakistani scholars tend to be more prescriptive than descriptive, so that empirical research for social analysis is often neglected. As a result, rural perspectives are neither well-articulated nor well-publicized.

In this chapter, I report on several events and perceptions extant in a village in the recently organized Okara district of Punjab. I studied this village intensively from 1977 to 1978, revisited it in 1979, and returned there again in the summer of 1983 for follow-up work.[2] I do not argue that what I found in this village is typical for all Pakistani villages. Such a claim is methodologically indefensible. All I have to offer are the perspectives of various villagers, details of observed and reported behavior, and analyses of several key situations in terms of their relationship to the national Islamization policy.

ISLAM IN VILLAGE LIFE

The village, Chakpur (a pseudonym), was founded fifty years ago as part of a canal colony. Ethnically, it is comprised of two main groups: one primarily engaged in agriculture as owner-cultivators, and the other as *seipi* (village service people). In 1977, the population of Chakpur was about fourteen hundred; in 1985, it was probably close to seventeen hundred. Village lands amount to eleven hundred acres of generally sandy soil irrigated mainly by tubewells first installed under programs of the Ayub Khan government. The main crops are wheat, rice, sugar cane, and cotton. Agricultural modernization is evident in the widespread, though tempered, use of new seeds and chemical fertilizers. There is usually a surplus of both grains and cash crops, which are marketed at nearby mills and government-controlled collection centers. The village, founded upon the *pattidari* tenure system, is dominated by the descendents of the twenty-four original land-share holders. These families constitute about one-third of all villagers. While seipis—cobblers, barbers, carpenters, and others—are dependent upon landowning families for their livelihood, there are not great discrepancies in wealth within the village. Two facts account for this. First, the average holding per landowning household is fairly small, with little variance; and second, skilled and semiskilled villagers can find reasonable part-time work in nearby towns.[3]

Chakpur is not isolated from the places and events surrounding it. A new road has been built to replace the dirt trail which had connected the village to the main tehsil road. Although the number is still relatively small, more and more people are working in nearby towns. Several villagers have gone to Lahore, one hundred miles and four hours away, to search for employment. Since my previous visit in 1979, the village has been electrified. Many villagers have radios and keep abreast of provincial and national developments. Two villagers have journeyed abroad to work as laborers in the Middle East. Several others continue to pursue this possibility.

Perceptions about Islamization with regard to rural areas coincide with the general images of rural-urban contrasts. There are two central, somewhat contrary images of Pakistan's rural populace held by both the urban literary elite and villagers themselves. In the first view, villagers are regarded as *jangli*—savage, illiterate, and unsophisticated. Applied to their religious behavior, this view represents villagers as superstitious, susceptible to the influence of fraudulent pirs, ignorant of Islamic law and theology, and prone to customs of Hindu origin. In the second view, villagers are seen as *siddha sada*—simple and straightforward. Translated into religious behavior, villagers are seen as pure and wholesome: steadfast believers who follow the way of Islam with full faith, vigor, and trust.[4]

These two images generate two alternative views of the relation of Islamization to rural and urban populations. In the first view, the goals of Islamization are construed as the education, civilization, and rationalization of uncontrolled and misdirected rural society. Islamization, as a rural policy, means bringing the city—the 'ulema, the madrasa, Islamic publications, etc.—to the village. In the second view, Islamization has a different goal. It may be seen as an attempt to purify society by bringing rural simplicity and faith in Islam, as found in villages, to the cities.[5] In Chakpur, both views have found expression in events since 1977.

When I lived in Chakpur in 1977–78, I had ample opportunity to observe and discuss various practices and attitudes related to Islam. Indeed, it was difficult not to, for upon my arrival the village *Sayyed* (descendant of the Prophet), in an effort to convert me, had the mosque loudspeaker redirected toward the hut I occupied opposite the mosque. At that time, the mosque was a rather simple one-room building, with a stylish facade of a type quite popular in the area. It had an open veranda, and electricity for the loudspeaker and a single light bulb. It was the only place in the village, save for a cotton gin and the tubewells, that was electrified.

The loudspeaker was used for the *azan* (call to prayer) and for public announcements. In addition, just about every morning before dawn, the Sayyed would deliver a stirring sermon in the direction of sleepy villagers. With his voice booming over the loudspeaker, sometimes for hours on end, he would exhort villagers to follow the ways of Islam and the Prophet. The sermons were generally in Urdu, occasionally in Punjabi. They were also liberally laced with readings from the Qur'an and Arabic and Persian commentaries. This made them quite difficult to understand, as most villagers spoke only Punjabi. Coming from a well-known family in the district, this Sayyed, who is also a pir and has several *murids* in the village, saw his attempt to promulgate the Islamic way of life as his duty. Indeed, the sermonizing was done on a directive from his pir.[6]

The Sayyed was quite frustrated by the villagers' lack of response to his exhortations. He regarded most of them as people without a *qanoon* (law): people who would lie, cheat, steal, and do all sorts of immoral things to each other.

The Sayyed was respected in Chakpur. He was regarded as a literate man of noble descent. He practiced *desi tibb* (traditional medicine), and many villagers were thankful for his treatment. If a group of men were playing cards (even if not for money), they would stop playing and sometimes put away the cards on the approach of the Sayyed in deference to his belief that what they were doing was gambling, and hence sinful. Still, in small get-togethers or in private conversation, he would often be the subject of mild chiding: he was regarded as someone who would get too worked up over his efforts and make too big a deal over things that didn't matter.

The village *maulvi* (religious teacher and practitioner) found himself in a similar position. Unlike the Sayyed, who had his own small landholding (albeit in another village), the maulvi was technically a village seipi, dependent upon produce from village lands set aside for the purpose of supporting him and his family. The maulvi was expected to teach village boys to read the Qur'an, attend to daily prayers, conduct Eid sacrifices, and do all the things maulvis are supposed to do to ensure that actions directed towards Allah are properly undertaken. Or, as villagers put it, to do all the Allah stuff *(Allah Allah karo).* In 1978, the maulvi was being criticized for not being attentive enough to his duties. Some villagers noted his pattern of lateness for prayers; others thought he was not doing a very good job in his teaching; and so on. At that time, the maulvi was not seen as an arbitor or judge of village conflicts. In one incident, a disagreement on the proper treatment of a landlord's hired hand, the villagers laughed at my suggestion that the principals and clan leaders consult the maulvi. The maulvi's knowledge of shariat law was deemed irrelevant for most important matters in village life, namely disputes and issues having to do with land, women, and wealth.

Another specialist in the village was an elderly widow who taught some of the village girls how to read the Qur'an. While the maulvi had eight to twelve boys to teach and was essentially being paid for his services, the widow had a smaller group of four to five students and taught them on her own initiative. I was aware of no major village event in 1979 at which she performed a key role because of her knowledge of Islam or her role as a teacher.

Other religious specialists deeply affecting village life were pirs. In 1978, just about every adult male had a pir. Pirs might serve as spiritual guides to their followers, or at least provide for the identification of villagers with one or another spiritual brotherhood. Villagers hosted the visits of several Gilani and Bukhari pirs. These visits were marked with music, feasting, and sermonizing. Several villagers were also quite active in visiting the various *khanqahs* (tombs) of pirs, as well as making visits to the more famous *darbars* (court or pilgrimage center) of Baba Farid in Pakpattan, Datta Ganj Baksh in Lahore, and Qadiri shrines in Multan. Accompanying various villagers on such trips, I found that sometimes these trips provided entertainment and allowed for sightseeing and adventure. At other times, they offered the opportunity for spiritual enhancement and deeply moving experiences.[7]

There was no question that villagers identified themselves as Muslims. Over 93 percent of the villagers had "Muslim" names as opposed to "secular Punjabi" names. In terms of Muslim behavior, however, village patterns presented a mixed bag. Of the whole population, perhaps four or five villagers would generally say *namaz* (ritual prayers) five times a day. Zakat and *sadqat* were given by a few, albeit landowners, on Eid. Occasionally such contributions—when intended for a publicly announced purpose—would be communicated over the mosque loudspeaker. Bakri Eid sacrifices were celebrated with relish and many families would join together in co-sponsoring the sacrifice of a water buffalo or a sheep. During Ramadan, I was absent from the village; however, interview data indicate that less than a handful of villagers kept the fast for the full month and that most adults fasted for perhaps five to ten days in 1979. As of that time, no villager had yet performed the hajj.

What has Islamization meant in Chakpur? The Zia government assumed control during my stay there in 1977. Have the attitudes and practices of villagers changed? Is an Islamic order more evident? Observing and interviewing villagers in Chakpur for more than three months in 1983, a rough assessment is possible.

As far as saying namaz, keeping the fast, and reading the Qur'an, the numbers of villagers performing these actions does not seem to have changed. At prayer times, the azan still sounds out over the village lands, but still only a handful of people join for namaz at the mosque. Neither in homes nor in field camps is there evidence of participation in prayer outside the mosque. Fasting during Ramadan is still held by all those I interviewed to be an enobling act, but many also find it a difficult one, especially when undertaken during a harsh summer by people forced to labor under trying circumstances. While many villagers said they would like to fast, they also said that conditions make fasting impossible to perform without jeopardizing their life and their health. Interestingly, no one, either in 1978 or in 1983, questioned the legitimacy of the fast itself, or its beneficial effects. These two points—the legitimacy of certain actions, and the circumstancial difficulties in their enactment—are common attitudes in Chakpur towards the performance of actions deemed "Islamic."

Taking another pillar of Islam, still no one has performed hajj or *umra*, although several villagers have presumably had the chance to do so.

The central government institution of shariat law has yet to affect villagers in a direct way. Hudud ordinances, discussed by villagers, have yet to be applied to villagers themselves. Generally, Chakpuris have been quite reluctant to adjudicate conflicts through the court system. Seeking the police, using lawyers, and being called before the court bring forth all sorts of intrusions most Chakpuris regard as undesirable. Most conflict resolution among villagers is handled informally through clan leaders (*biradari*, heads), or by public argument. Using the courts is really a last resort, done only when the local machinery for resolving a disagreement has broken down. This happened the first time I was in the village, when a murder was committed. Often, though, relatively severe conflicts never reach the courts. For example, one villager having a long-term affair with the wife of a fellow clansman was continually upbraided by delegations of influential intermediaries, but was never the subject of an official police complaint, even though he freely acknowledged the affair.

This last case has provided a focus for many in discussing the hudud ordinances. There are perhaps as many as a dozen fairly well-known long-term adulterous affairs in progress in Chakpur. Villagers generally regard themselves as very excitable people with strong sexual urges and desires. To many, the ordinances concerning adultery and fornication are overly harsh considering human nature and the prevailing temperaments of Chakpuris. Given the "uncontrollable" nature of such urges and desires, it is difficult for many to understand the severity of hudud punishments. Besides, many say, sexual affairs are enjoyable, and, at least for many village men, provide a focus for much storytelling and joke-making.

Islamization does not appear to have affected the status of village specialists dealing with religious belief and action. The maulvi is still the subject of criticism in the village. He has not gained any arbitration or assessment powers there. Problems concerning such things as compensation for work or punishments for indiscretions are solved without recourse to the maulvi's advice, and certainly without explicit reference to any Qur'anic source.

The village Sayyed is still frustrated. In his words, the other villagers are still like animals, *janglis* without manners, knowledge, or propriety. He still delivers his sermons to a sleeping audience, and continues to exhort them to wake up and behave like good Muslims. While he is still chided for his intensity and serious demeanor, he is nonetheless respected. In Pakistan, attitudes towards mullahs are often ambivalent, and those towards the Sayyed in Chakpur are no exception. Villagers continue to play cards and loud music, to his consternation, but also continue to temper their behavior in his presence.

The widow more than anyone else has gained in status under the new regime. She was selected to the district council as the women's representative. Because of her position, the village has been targeted for various development efforts. Her selection was the result of several factors: she was left in control of a relatively large amount of land; she had fairly powerful relatives; she was a post-menopausal female; and she had a reputation for piety and service. While the new regime has provided the means for her rise to power, she might have done just as well under any other regime. Also, the particular Islamization platform of the present government may have had very little to do with her selection. A platform favoring women's rights, moral leadership, or even a popular election might have done just as well.

ISLAMIZATION AND VILLAGE ISSUES

There are three issues in Chakpur which have assumed some prominence during the course of my work, and provide a focus for many of the thoughts about Islamization in the village: the banning of opium; the imposition of 'ushr; and the expansion of the village mosque.

The Banning of Opium

Several of the villagers were lifelong users of opium and hashish. Soon after coming to power, Zia ul-Haq ordered closed previously licensed opium shops, hence cutting the legitimate supply to consumers. While in some parts of the country, particularly urban areas and the frontier, addicts may have had continued access, the ban hit village addicts particularly hard.

The government did allow an interim period during which village addicts could receive a medicinal substitute from an authorized hospital or clinic. But for Chakpuri addicts, the distance they had to travel and the lack of satisfaction they received from the substitute mitigated the possible effectiveness of the program.

Of the several addicts in the village, two were relatively well-off landowners. While their addiction—well known to all—was not something held up as an object of pride, neither was it something inviting the scorn or moral umbrage of their neighbors. After the ban, villagers had a chance to see its effect upon their neighbors. People who had been addicted to opium for twenty or thirty years did not do well in a cold-turkey withdrawal. Villagers were aware of their suffering, and many empathized with their plight. One former addict died within several months of the ban. Others survived. One survivor notes that he has endured and conquered his addiction. He doesn't feel redeemed, however. By no means does he feel it made him more moral, a better Muslim, or anything of the sort. He did it because he had to. Other former addicts have also adapted: many continue to use less powerful but locally available drugs. Generally, village consensus seems to be that forcing people to do something, and causing pain to those in difficult circumstances, does not necessarily result in moral uplift or a rejuvenation of religious feelings. In short, forcing abstinance was painful and did not have any moral implications for village addicts.

The Imposition of 'Ushr

Zia's regime imposed payment of 'ushr upon various classes of landlords. In Chakpur, the assessment of 'ushr was to take place during the 1982 wheat harvest, but as of the summer of 1983 it had still not been finalized. Plans in the works call for the taxation of many who heretofore had legitimately avoided taxes.

Prior to the institutionalization of 'ushr, gift-giving for charity and village level projects occurred fairly informally under the control of biradari and clan leaders. The worthiness of the project needing money would be assessed by various *maliks*—generally landowning leaders of families, *pattis* (shareholders), and clans. On their approval, an effort would be launched to solicit funds, or in some cases labor, from other villagers. Appeals and donations might be announced over the loudspeaker. While pressures to give would exist, they were largely of a face-to-face, personal nature. Cooperation, competition, considerations of pride, honor, jealousy, and service might be invoked to solicit aid.

The Zia government's imposition of zakat on bank accounts and 'ushr on agricultural produce was widely resented by villagers for several reasons. First, it was taken to be just another tax, raising the expense of an already marginal agricultural production enterprise. Second, the results of such contributions were not clear; villagers did not want to pay for unspecified services or projects. Third, the tax was imposed by the regime and was therefore not voluntary. Hence, villagers argued, it would hardly be paid from a feeling of Islamic duty. The use of compulsion to evoke charitable contributions was not something the villagers regarded as in accord with the nobler aspirations of Islam.

Villagers pointed with pride to the voluntary contributions they made to village welfare before such payments were imposed by law and thought of them as being more in accordance with Islam. "Islam," to be effective, must be voluntary, not forced, argued villagers. In addition, villagers argued that zakat and 'ushr can work in a society that is Islamic, with a government that is just and citizenry that does its duty. But, they argued, Pakistani society is not Islamic, government officials not always just, and citizens not always sincere and worthy. Rather, in an un-Islamic society, it is misappropriated funds, a government beyond their control, incomprehensible and inaccessible institutions, and a world of bribes and scams that colored Chakpuri visions of the world beyond their village. Zakat and 'ushr were likely to be misappropriated in such a system, they believed. Various people were liable to misuse and steal such funds. The wrong people might get the benefits of such contributions. And wealthy people would be likely to escape having to pay. In short, Chakpuris perceived the implementation of a fair, honest, and moral system as an impossibility in the context of present-day Pakistan.

The Mosque Expansion Project

While villagers tended to be very skeptical of government "Islamization," they were not skeptical about Islam. Islam is a continuing source of legitimation for Chakpuris: it is their knowledge of the natural world; it is the code underpinning their customs; it is the basis of the moral principles parents attempt to teach their children. If something is thought to be good or moral, it is taken to be part of Islam. If something is thought to be correct, right, or true about the natural order of things, it is taken to be part of Islam. All this is irrespective of what is in the Qur'an or commentaries or hadith or fiqh or sunnah. Islam for Chakpuris is not a specific set of particular laws about such things as punishment, inheritance, economics, or statecraft. It is not the specifics that color the maulvi's knowledge or the Sayyed's sermons, for in these specifics, Chakpuris find all sorts of ambiguities and contradictions which they attempt to work around: inheritance for daughters, observing fasts, and saying daily prayers, for example. Islam to them is rather a symbol of the good, the correct, the moral, and the right. When one is a good man in village parlance, one is by definition a good Muslim. Indeed, Islam is the only symbol of morality, justice, and truth. Appeals to manmade codes, constitutions, or institutions, or to some appreciation of human nature do not provide satisfactory bases of legitimacy in Chakpur. On this, there is strong villagewide consensus, for in identifying themselves as Muslims, Chakpuris express their legitimacy as a human community endowed with the grace of Allah.

The unity of the village, and its goodness, are expressed through the mosque. Just about all villagers have donated money, labor, or materials for its maintenance. Since 1977, the size of the village mosque has more than doubled. Villagers paid for and worked to build a large addition and a beautiful hand-crafted minaret. Chakpuris are proud of their effort. It indicates that they are good people, able to work as a cooperative and brotherly community of Muslims.

The villagers could have collectively invested their time, money, labor, and materials in productive resources—livestock, a village tractor, or spraying equipment, for example—or in consumer goods—a television set, modern baths, a refrigerator or fancy cassette tape player—but they did not. Such goods tend to be those owned and transmitted through families. Investment in the mosque transcends such products and individual family ties. The mosque serves as the objectification of a spiritual unity which makes the village a community. As they have apparently done in the past, members of this community have sought to articulate their communal identity as a particularly Muslim one at a time when it makes eminent political sense to do so. Although they may not accept the policies of the government Islamization program, Chakpuris do not want to be disadvantaged in doing so, and certainly do not want to be labelled "bad" or "sinful" Muslims as well.

BEYOND CHAKPUR

What happens to Chakpuris who venture beyond the village to tehsil, district, and provincial towns? Does their notion of Islam and Islamization change, and if so, how? Several Chakpuris and people from a neighboring village have had this experience, and three general types of reactions can be described.

In the first situation, some villagers settled in a nearby town. They live in a relatively isolated block of homes and interact predominantly within their own circle of kin. They maintain close ties to the village and its traditional leaders, including their pirs. Although they live in the town, they have not made much of an effort, nor have they been forced, to encounter the plural currents of Islamic beliefs and practices of their neighbors. In short, their discourse with regard to Islamic issues seems no different than their village brethren.

For other Chakpuris who have gone to the city and been exposed to a variety of linguistic and ethnic groups practicing other variants of Sunni, Shi'a, Ismaili, and Ahmediya ways, the experience has been quite different. Some Chakpuris with such experience speak of the different, often discordant, and sometimes contradictory views of the maulvis, Sayyeds, and pirs they have encountered. To such thoughtful villagers, this variety necessitates some contemplation, discrimination, and judgment. Issues must be discussed and arguments made. Notions of correct and incorrect positions and interpretations are formulated. For these Chakpuris, the fact that there is more than one way, that variation among Muslims exists, and that practices and beliefs can be, and actively are, questioned, is of tremendous importance. Insofar as they participate in the questioning and confrontation of their own practice of Islam, such villagers find themselves doing precisely what they often characterize urbanites as doing: using their rational faculty *('aql)* in the service of spirituality *(ruh).* By their own definition, they become more sophisticated. Islamization thus entails the rationalization of more simple "folk" beliefs and practices, through exposure to public debate, sermons, education, and the media.

An alternative experience is, however, probably more common. To many of those villagers who settle in cities, the variation in the norms of Islam and the discourse about it is taken as a distortion of a more unified reality. In this case, the villager laughs at the supposedly knowledgable urbanites who argue endlessly over trivial points. Long and detailed theological debates on the question of precisely where to cut the hand of a thief seem to him pointless. In this view, city people use their rational faculty not to enhance spirituality, but rather to obfuscate it. To the villager, one's "Muslimness" is felt as a "natural" basic feature of one's identity. The urbanite, from this perspective, is making an issue out of this identity, and hence complicating it unnecessarily. In this view, Islamization is seen as bringing village notions to the city, stripping away the folly of human rationalization and manipulation, and substituting in its stead a more straightforward acceptance and faith.

CONCLUSION

Villagers do not see themselves as participants in the present explicit government Islamization effort. This is so for several reasons. First, they do not identify with government efforts in general. The government, including the present one, has always been viewed from a distance with a good deal of apprehension and suspicion. Moreover, the present Islamization effort, like previous efforts, is an imposed program. It is not understandable to many. It is impractical. It ignores the circumstances and realities of village life, and for that matter, a rural view of human nature and Pakistani society. Second, in a fundamental way, Chakpuris do not accept the assumptions the present regime is making about the relationship between the government and Islam. For the government, Pakistan is a nation of Muslims and therefore "should be" an Islamic state. For Chakpuris, Pakistan as a land for Muslims means a nation in which Muslims, as people, are in control. It means that they, as Muslims, have protected rights to their lands, their livelihoods, and their families. Pakistan as a nation of mullahs or scholars or ideologues would be quite impractical in Chakpuri terms, just as the Sayyed, the maulvi, and even revered pirs do not generate the basic resources (women, wealth, and land) for survival in the village. The present government, its policies, its pronouncements and expectations, are just too ideological and too impractical for Chakpuris.

This is not to say that Chakpuris are un- or non-Islamic. They view themselves as Islamic, but in different terms. They did not have to expand the mosque and incur substantial expenses; they did so voluntarily. They support the village maulvi, respect the Sayyed, and adore their pirs. Those are the ways in which they define themselves as part of a larger human community that is indeed moral. Although they do this on a daily basis, the need for such identification is heightened at certain times of the year—for example, during festivals—and in the face of certain political situations, both historically and currently. Clearly in terms of international events, vocal and articulate Chakpuris assert their "Muslimness" when speaking of India, Sikhs, and Hindus; the Middle East; United States policy; Israel; the Islamic bomb; and so on. Islam is for them an expression of identity, an idiom of and for morality, and a source of legitimacy. It is viewed as an object, a core symbol, and not as a specific theology, philosophy, body of practice, set of moral injunctions or legal doctrines, and certainly not as a social order promulgated by the current government.

NOTES

1. An earlier version of this chapter appeared in *Asian Survey* 25, No. 8 (August 1985): 852–62.

2. Research from 1976–78 was sponsored by grants from the U.S. Office of Education, the Fulbright-Hays program, and the Social Science Research Council. Research during 1983 was sponsored by the American Institute of Pakistan Studies.

3. See Richard Kurin, "Person, Family and Kin in Two Pakistani Communities" (Doctoral dissertation, Department of Anthropology, University of Chicago, 1981), and Kurin, "Indigenous Agronomics and Agricultural Development," *Human Organization* 42, No. 4: 283–94, for extended descriptions of Chakpur.

4. See Richard Kurin, "The Culture of Ethnicity in Two Pakistani Communities" in *South Asian Islam: Moral Principles in Tension*, ed. Katharine Ewing (Berkeley: University of

California Press, forthcoming). See also Barbara D. Metcalf, "Introduction" in *Moral Conduct and Authority: The Place of Adab in South Asian Islam* ed. Barbara Metcalf (Berkeley: University of California Press, 1984).

5. See Ira Lapidus, "Knowledge, Virtue and Action" in Metcalf, *Moral Conduct and Authority.*

6. For an account of this pir, see Katherine Ewing, "The Politics of Sufism: Redefining the Saints of Pakistan," *Journal of Asian Studies* 42, No. 2 (February 1983): 251–67).

7. For a description of a shrine visited by Chakpuris, see Richard Eaton, "The Political and Religious Authority of the Shrine of Baba Farid" in *Moral Conduct and Authority*, ed. Barbara Metcalf.

8

The Political Meaning of Islamization in Pakistan: Prognosis, Implications, and Questions

William L. Richter

The role of Islam, after some eclipse during the Ayub and early Bhutto years, has once again become a central issue in Pakistan's political, social, and economic life.[1] The current military regime of General Zia ul-Haq has implemented a variety of reforms ostensibly designed to establish a true *Nizam-i-Islam* (Islamic rule). The features of many of those reforms—in the legal system, economy, election rules, administrative practices, and other sectors of society—have been discussed in considerable detail in the foregoing essays and elsewhere.[2] In the various commentaries on Islamization in Pakistan which have thus far appeared, there are a number of recurring themes, including the following sets of questions:

1. How did Islamization come about in Pakistan? To what extent is Islamization a genuine social movement rooted in Pakistan's Islamic heritage and to what extent is it, conversely, a cynical exploitation of Islam to lend legitimacy to an unrepresentative military dictatorship? To what extent is Islamization merely a ploy to keep the military in power?
2. What have been the consequences of Islamization in Pakistan? What impact have reforms had upon the society?
3. What is the future of Islamization in Pakistan? Are the current reforms merely a passing fad or are they likely to be a

> permanent feature of Pakistani life? How permanent will the changes be if the military is removed from control? What are the bases of political support for and opposition to Islamization in Pakistan?

Several of the essays in this volume deal explicitly or implicitly with one or more of these questions. This concluding chapter is an attempt both to review and integrate some of these earlier observations and to suggest some additional considerations.

ORIGINS

To some, government Islamization efforts are simply the culmination of a gradual increase in Muslim consciousness. Viewed this way, the movement for a separate state of Pakistan and the resultant state are simply earlier milestones in an ongoing process. Weiss's introduction to this volume outlines much of this Islamic legacy. Pakistan, it is argued by President Zia and others, was created as an Islamic country and Islamization is merely the fulfillment of that heritage.

Several writings, including Alavi's essay in this volume, take serious issue with this interpretation, however.[3] They point out that the Muslim League under Jinnah's leadership was a secular movement which was strongly opposed before Partition by the groups which later came to advocate the Islamization of Pakistan.

Despite the apparent historical accuracy of this argument, the circumstances surrounding Pakistan's creation, including the raising of Muslim consciousness, provided a pool of potent symbols on which Islamic groups could later draw. The irony, as Alavi shows, was that these symbols were most heavily exploited by those who had opposed the creation of Pakistan. This phenomenon was most clearly manifested in the extensive debates in the Pakistan Constituent Assembly over the Objectives Resolution,[4] but it also found expression in the anti-Ahmediya riots of 1953, the formal designation of Pakistan as an "Islamic Republic" in the Constitutions of 1956 and 1962, the appointment of an Islamic Ideology Council, and other measures.[5]

After the 1971 civil war, Islam appeared to decline as a political issue in Pakistan.[6] By the late 1970s, however, this trend had been reversed. Islam and Islamic reform became central issues in Pakistani political discourse. How is this "resurgence" or "reassertion" to be explained?

Hamza Alavi and others argue that the object of Islamization is "not 'Islam' but rather that of invoking a claim to state power as an alternative to restoration of representative government." From this perspective, Islamic reforms are a clever device to mobilize popular support, especially among those whom Alavi calls "the mullahs and the bigots," and to divert attention from issues of representative versus authoritarian rule.

As Weiss notes in the Preface, however, Islamization was "not simply a scheme dreamed up overnight by a military government to appease a hostile populace." Explanation of Islam's renewed prominence in the 1970s as a political issue requires consideration of a variety of factors.[7]

First, Pakistani society appears to have been made much more susceptible to Islamic appeals by (a) the trauma of the Bangladesh war and the identity crisis which accompanied the loss of the eastern half of the country; (b) the increased prominence and power of the Islamic countries of the Middle East during the 1970s; and (c) disillusionment with foreign ideologies as they had been manifested in Pakistan: first capitalism under Ayub Khan and later Bhutto's brand of socialism.

Secondly, the pressure for infusing Islamic values into government, society, and the economy was visible in the "Nizam-i-Mustafa" slogans of the Pakistan National Alliance campaign in the March 1977 elections—several months before the military seized power. The dynamics of coalition-building among the diverse parties of this alliance made Islam a useful slogan, sufficiently potent to elicit public support. What the PNA tapped then, and Zia has been able to use since, is an underlying public sympathy to Islam sufficient to endure Pakistan's longest period of martial law and some of the fairly radical political and social changes which the current regime has brought about.

Even Zulfikar Ali Bhutto recognized the public appeal of Islamic issues and instituted several reforms in April 1977, three months before his overthrow. Among other things, this "defensive Islamization" changed the weekly holiday from Sunday to Friday and outlawed horseracing and the drinking of alcoholic beverages.

The military regime's sponsorship of Islamic reforms then is a product of a political and social environment that preceded by several years the July 1977 coup. Still, the military might not have chosen to emphasize Islamization had the symbols of Islam not coincided so well with General Zia's own fundamentalist religious values and his class and family ties to the Jama'at-i-Islami.

During the early months following Bhutto's overthrow, the initial goals of the military regime were rapidly supplanted by Islamization as a central goal.[8] The initial justification of the 5 July coup, that of holding fair elections and returning power to civilian leaders, rapidly became untenable when the generals realized that the results of popular elections would be detrimental to their interests, and possibly to their lives. A second goal, that of "accountability" for past wrongdoing, quickly lost its potency once Bhutto had been hanged in April 1979. Unlike either of these goals, Islamization is sufficiently vague and diffuse to last a long time as a political issue, yet sufficiently rooted in Pakistan's history and culture to compel considerable public support.

Perhaps the clearest example of the military exploitation of the religious issue was General Zia's nationwide referendum of 19 December 1984. In the referendum, the voters were asked to indicate "whether they supported the process initiated by the Government for the Islamization of all laws in accordance with the Holy Qur'an and Sunnah and whether they supported the Islamic ideology of Pakistan."[9] The government severely proscribed any vocal opposition to the referendum. Even advocacy of a boycott of the vote was made a punishable crime. At the same time, General Zia toured the country campaigning for public support of the proposal. Despite considerable skepticism from critics, the government claimed that 60 percent of the eligible population voted and that 97.7 percent of the valid votes were cast in favor of the regime and its Islamization program. General Zia interpreted the referendum results as a mandate to remain in office for another five years and to continue the processes of social, political, and economic change he had initiated.

In summary, it appears that Islamization in Pakistan has entailed military exploitation, but that the military is not the only group which has exploited Islam for political benefits. Certainly Bhutto attempted to do so, as have the various Islam-oriented parties. Islamization is seen largely as a function of political dynamics, of which military exploitation of the Islamic issue is only one aspect.

Whatever their origins and objectives, the actions of the present regime have created an atmosphere and institutions which may continue in Pakistan long after military rule has ended. The extent to which such developments persist will depend upon both the nature of the specific reforms and the pace and process by which the military exits from politics.

IMPACT AND CONSEQUENCES

The reassertion of Islamic values in Pakistan, as in other areas of the Muslim world, has had a widespread and diverse social and political impact. As this volume's introductory essay and other accounts show, major legal, economic, and social changes have been wrought by Islamic reform measures. New rules and new institutions have been developed for the administration of justice, economic investment, and the collection and distribution of special taxes for social welfare purposes (zakat).

Perhaps more far-reaching than the specific Islamic laws and programs has been the changed public atmosphere. In many respects, Islam has come to define the parameters of political discourse. This is dictated to some degree by the martial law regulations which provided severe punishments for the utterance of public statements against the regime, the military, or Pakistan's Islamic ideology. But the renewed public concern over Islamic principles has also unleashed a considerable amount of creative endeavor in a variety of areas, as many of the contributions in this volume show.

Several of the studies in this volume deal specifically with the application and impact of the various reforms under the present regime. In many respects, they show that Islamization in Pakistan has been less thoroughgoing in practice than in rhetoric. Richard Kurin notes that village life in Chakpur has not changed dramatically with the implementation of Islamic reforms. As Weiss adds, shari'a courts have been established, but their jurisdiction under martial law has been restricted and they have been specifically forbidden to question the actions of the military authorities. The government has established its zakat program with implementation machinery from the national to the village level, but, as Clark shows, much of that machinery remains inoperable at the lower levels of the system.

Viewed more positively, the government has taken a relatively pragmatic approach toward Islamization, as Burki notes in his chapter. The changes, he argues, "will be slow and subtle and perhaps permanent."

As several observers have noted, Islamization's impact in Pakistan is likely to be affected by the nature of the reforms which are pursued. It is possible to deduce from Islam a political and legal system based upon equality and consent. The values of social concern, represented by the practice of zakat, of the legal rights of women, of justice and equality, are all to be found in Islam. Although some of these values (such as zakat) have been translated into Islamization programs in Pakistan, the more prominent features of the program have served to reinforce authoritarian control. The use of flogging as a punishment, even for the voicing of political opinions, has helped subdue opposition to military rule. Even the zakat system, as Mayer and Clark show, has served to provide the government with both a valuable revenue source and an important patronage and support structure.

Most controversial, perhaps, have been those features of Islamization which have affected the role and status of women in Pakistani society, as Weiss shows us. From restrictions on women's sports to the dress code for those women who appear on television, to new legal provisions which define a woman as having half the credibility and half the value of a man,[10] many women see Islamization as an attack upon what few gains they had made before the military returned to power in 1977. The most militant of the women's groups, the Women's Action Forum, was formed during the martial law period and has actively attempted both to lobby and to agitate against Islamic reforms based upon Qur'anic interpretations prejudicial to women.

Religious minorities have also been affected by the increasing emphasis upon Islamization. The Ahmediyas, or Qadianis as they are commonly known, were the object of riots in 1953 and 1974. They found themselves constitutionally defined out of the community of Islam in 1974 and further restricted in their religious practices in 1984, because of their belief that their nineteenth-century founder, Mirza Ghulam Ahmed, was a latter-day prophet. In response to pressures from *khatm-i-nabuwwat* (finality of prophethood) societies throughout Pakistan, Zia issued orders in 1984 forbidding the Ahmediyas to call themselves Muslims, to preach to Muslims, to call their place of worship a *masjid* (mosque), or to utilize such Islamic religious practices as the azan (call to prayer). To a lesser degree, but with a larger population base, the minority Shi'a community has also feared domination by the majority Sunni population and has attempted to ensure that Islamization does not simply result in the codification of Sunni interpretations of Islam. Shi'as have occasionally found it necessary to agitate for inclusion of their variants of Islamic reforms, as in the issue of criminal punishment. They have pressed, so far in vain, for governmental recognition of their own legal code, fiqh Jafaria.

Most of the commentary on the consequences of Islamization, in this volume and elsewhere, treats the question in terms of the impact of reforms upon society. The discussion here has suggested in several ways that that impact, though substantial and potentially far-reaching, may be less dramatic at present than the rhetoric of proponents—or the fears of opponents—might imply.

Mayer's study raises another interesting impact question: what are the likely consequences of Islamization for Islam itself? The transformation of personal duties such as zakat into legally enforced obligations, the conduct of prayers in government offices, the designation of dress codes, and the enforcement of fasting during Ramadan all modify the nature of the relation between the Muslim, Islam, and the state. Just as the villagers of Chakpur felt that compliance with new government regulations stemming from Islamic reforms did not make them any better Muslims, so other Pakistanis might well question what consequences coercive enforcement of Islamic rules might have for Islam. As governmental programs and institutions become more Islamic, is Islam likely to become more depersonalized, desectarianized, and governmental?

SUPPORT, OPPOSITION, AND THE FUTURE OF ISLAMIZATION IN PAKISTAN

What is the future of Islamization in Pakistan? General Zia has frequently suggested that the Islamic reforms which have already taken place are only the beginning steps in a journey toward a fully Islamic political, economic, and social system. If this rhetoric is to be believed, then one might expect the future pace of Islamic reforms to remain steady and even to increase. Few observers hold such expectations, however.

Even Zia's own assessment, as of mid-summer 1985, was much less expectantly optimistic than earlier public statements would imply. When asked about the success of his Islamization program, he initially responded, "It has been a failure," then corrected himself and said, "It has not entirely been a success." The problem, he explained, lay in persuading other Pakistanis who did not see the issues as he did. Using political parties as an example, he said it would be wrong to impose his view upon a country which saw matters differently from him. He still felt there was no place for political parties in an Islamic polity, and would continue to voice his opinions, but he could see that a lot of good Muslims regarded parties as both necessary and compatible with Islam.[11]

Burki, looking at economic planning, suggests that future Islamic reforms are likely to be relatively slow and subtle, but perhaps more permanent as a result of their more deliberate pace. Alavi, on the other hand, argues that the Islamization process has possibly reached an impasse because Zia has promised more than he can deliver. It would seem, at least, that the most obvious Islamic reforms, and the ones with greatest dramatic or symbolic value, have already been made and that much of the future Islamization effort will be directed at implementation and incremental or marginal change.

If the dynamics of Islamic reassertion in the past have depended upon the vagaries of Pakistani politics, as several chapters in this volume argue, then we might expect that the future of Islamization will also be tied to the fate of political developments which are presently under way in Pakistan.

There obviously has been opposition to Zia and, less vocally, to Islamization. The officially outlawed component parties of the Movement for the Restoration of Democracy (MRD), particularly the Pakistan People's Party, regard much of the Islamization package as a set of devices intended to perpetuate military rule and destroy whatever bases of representative government have been established in Pakistan. After the lifting of martial law the Pakistan People's Party, led by a forceful Benazir Bhutto, has called for new elections and a return to the 1973 Constitution which Zia has heavily modified by fiat. Bhutto's Pakistan People's Party is a major component of the Movement for the Restoration of Democracy, but by no means the only element. Many of the parties which were in the anti-Bhutto Pakistan National Alliance in 1977 are today in the anti-Zia Movement for the Restoration of Democracy. Faced in the 1984 referendum with an obviously one-sided contest, the Movement called for a boycott and claimed afterward that no more than 5 percent of the voting public had turned out to cast ballots. However, extensive government control of the media and willingness to use arrests and other forms of coercion sufficed to minimize the political influence of the Movement for the Restoration of Democracy both before and after the referendum. In general, the Movement has consistently been overpowered and outmaneuvered by the Zia regime. Its most serious challenge to Zia came in late 1983, when Sindhi regional discontent was fanned into several weeks of violent anti-government protest. The failure of the protest to extend into other provinces, particularly into Punjab, left the Movement in disarray, exhausted, and with an even more ineffectual image than before. Even the Movement for the Restoration of Democracy, it should be noted, has been reluctant to make direct criticism of the policy of Islamization.

The parties to the right of the Movement have been even more reluctant to raise objections either to Zia's rule or to Islamization. The two most prominent of these, the Jama'at-i-Islami and the Pakistan Muslim League of Pir Pagaro, have at times been openly supportive of the present government. Even these groups, however, have occasionally questioned the good faith and intentions of General Zia. The Jama'at has expressed fears that the military's use of Islam to keep itself in office will give Islam a bad name. Jama'at support for Zia probably reached its low point in the spring of 1984, when the government banned student political organizations from college and university campuses. Since the Jama'at-i-Tulaba, the student wing of the Jama'at, has dominated student politics on many campuses, this was a direct blow to the support base of political parties generally and of the Jama'at-i-Islami in particular.

The most vocal opposition to Islamization has come from women's groups, but their resistance has largely focused on discontent over specific issues rather than a broader questioning of either the ideology or the overall program of Islamization. Without a tradition of church-state separation, such as that which in the United States has helped to temper the political claims of Christian fundamentalism, and in the face of such committed and visible Islamic fundamentalists as Dr. Israr Ahmed and the Jama'at-i-Islami, women have found it difficult to arouse much public support for their position.

Several writers have attached the label "Bonapartist" to Pakistan's present regime and to some of its predecessors.[12] Following Marx's argument in *The Eighteenth Brumaire of Louis Napoleon Bonaparte*, a Bonapartist regime is one which does not rest on a single class base but rather manipulates all significant classes through symbolic or real rewards. The state is thereby able to establish a relative autonomy from the control of any single class or social group. General Zia has clearly shown his ability to manipulate those who expected to manipulate him. Pir Pagaro of the Pakistan Muslim League and other party politicians who expected to ride to power on military coattails in 1977 found their parties outlawed in 1979 and themselves either in a political wilderness or indebted to Zia's new political order by 1985. The 'ulema who expected Islamization to usher in a system in which they might play a major role have seen the military co-opt their issues and remain in charge. Even some of the military officers who saw Zia as an easily manipulated front man for their own behind-the-scenes power plays have found themselves squeezed from power by Zia's periodic shakeups of his top military councils.

Zia has assiduously sought to build a diversity of support constituencies, of which the Islamic base is only one. Moreover, this Islamic "bloc," as Alavi has shown, is greatly fragmented among several significant groupings: the Jama'at-i-Islami; other competing parties of 'ulema (e.g., the Jamiat-i-ulema-i-Pakistan and the Jamiat-i-ulema-i-Islam); the many pirs and *makhdums* (caretakers of religious shrines); and others. In addition to these, Zia has generated support among much of the business community by eliminating the specter of nationalization which Bhutto had spread, and because of Pakistan's relatively robust economy since the military takeover. Although some of the bureaucrats have been somewhat angered by the widespread appointment of both serving and retired military officers to bureaucratic positions, several higher bureaucrats have been given key policy-making positions.

Yet another constituency has been developed through Zia's new political institutions, beginning with the re-activation of local government councils in 1979 and the later appointment of the Majlis-e-Shura (Federal

Consultative Council) and provincial councils. Since August 1983, General Zia has been pursuing a plan of restoring civilian government in Pakistan through cooptation, nonpartisan elections, and a gradual sharing of power with the elected civilians. Despite delays and diversions, that plan is still in the process of being implemented. In February 1985, national and provincial elections were held. Although the elections were held on a nonparty basis and opponents were restrained from publicizing their call for a boycott, the polls were generally regarded as fair and well-attended.[13] Martial law was officially lifted on 31 December 1985 and limited political activity permitted to resume.

We can at this point project two major scenarios which might flow from these developments. The first, and perhaps more promising, is the continued gradual civilianization of politics on the basis of the 1985 elections. Both Zia and the civilian politicians now in office agree that relatively rapid movement in this direction is both desirable and essential if the process is to retain credibility. The major potential problem with this process is that it leaves the MRD politicians out of the equation, at least for the time being. The latter have generally been willing to watch from the sidelines, expecting some slip in Zia's orchestrated plan.

What are the implications for Islamization? First, it is likely to decrease in importance for several reasons. The civilian politicians are themselves generally not as enthusiastic for Islamic reforms as General Zia has been. As Alavi has shown, few of the representatives of the Islamic parties were elected in the 1985 elections. Those who were elected, though no doubt willing to voice their loyalties to Islamic principles, are less likely to be as zealous in proposing new reforms. On the other hand, a gradual transition from military to civilian rule will help to legitimize those Islamic reforms which have already taken place, in effect consolidating the "Islamic revolution" which the military regime has sponsored.

The alternative scenario would be the possible breakdown and frustration of the present civilianization process and the reimposition of strict military rule. There are several possible conditions under which such a scenario might unfold. One would be a confrontation between the elected assembly and the president, especially if it involved a threat to military interests. Another would be the escalation of protest by the MRD and other unrepresented political forces which have been quite vocal since martial law restrictions were lifted. In the short run at least, either disruption in the orderly process of change, if sufficiently threatening, would almost certainly result in a reimposition of military control. Here the results for Islamization would probably be two-fold: first, a short-term increase in the regime's emphasis upon Islam, but, secondly, an increasing public alienation from both military rule and military policies, including Islamization. In the long run, such an eventuality would probably discredit Islamic reforms and possibly produce the sort of anti-Islamic reaction which occurred in the early 1970s.

CONCLUSIONS

Islamization in Pakistan draws upon a rich historical and religious heritage, but is in many respects a relatively recent phenomenon. It has developed in large part out of a specific but diverse set of political conditions in the 1970s and remains heavily dependent upon the dynamics of Pakistani politics.

The formulation, promulgation, and application of new Islamic laws have required a considerable amount of deliberation, planning, and institution-building, particularly with respect to economic and legal institutions.

However thoroughgoing Islamic reforms were intended to be, their application has not fully spread to the peripheries of Pakistani society. Rather, indifference among villagers and others, as well as resistance and reaction among women's groups and religious minorities, indicates that the fully Islamic system envisioned by General Zia and his supporters is hardly yet a reality. Nonetheless, major changes have occurred in several significant spheres of society.

Whether these changes will survive the end of military rule, whether future leaders will continue to press Islamization, and whether the people of Pakistan will continue to give political support to Islamic programs are questions which can be raised at this point, but which will only be answered as Pakistan's current political drama unfolds.

NOTES

1. Among the various accounts of this phenomenon, in addition to those cited later, are Anwar Hussain Syed, *Pakistan: Islam, Politics, and National Solidarity* (New York: Praeger, 1982); Edward Mortimer, *Faith and Power: The Politics of Islam* (New York: Random House, 1982), 186–229; Mumtaz Ahmad, "Parliament, Parties, Polls and Islam: Issues in the Current Debate on Religion and Politics in Pakistan," *American Journal of Islamic Social Sciences* 2, No. 1 (July 1985): 15–28; Lucy Carroll, "Nizam-i-Islam: Processes and Conflicts in Pakistan's Programme of Islamisation, with Special Reference to the Position of Women," *Journal of Commonwealth and Comparative Politics* 20 (1982): 57–95.

2. William L. Richter, "Pakistan" in *The Politics of Islamic Reassertion*, ed. Mohammad Ayoob (London: Croom Helm, 1981), 141–62.

3. Cf. Muhammad Munir, *From Jinnah to Zia* (Lahore: Vanguard Books, 1979); Hassan N. Gardezi, "The Resurgence of Islam: Islamic Ideology and Encounters with Imperialism," and Ziaul Haque, "Pakistan and Islamic Ideology," both in *Pakistan: The Roots of Dictatorship*, ed. Hassan Gardezi and Jamil Rashid (London: Zed Press, 1983), 353–66 and 367–83.

4. Leonard Binder, *Religion and Politics in Pakistan* (Berkeley: University of California Press, 1961).

5. See Freeland Abbott, *Islam and Pakistan* (Ithaca: Cornell University Press, 1968).

6. Khurshid Hyder, "Pakistan Under Bhutto," *Current History*, 63, No. 375 (November 1972): 202.

7. This argument is developed in greater detail in William L. Richter, "The Political Dynamics of Islamic Resurgence in Pakistan, *Asian Survey* 19, No. 6 (June 1979): 547–57.

8. Cf. William L. Richter, "Persistent Praetorianism: Pakistan's Third Military Regime," *Pacific Affairs* 51, No. 3 (Fall 1978), 406–26.

9. *Pakistan Times Overseas Weekly*, 9 December 1984, 1, 3.

10. Cf. Jamal Rasheed, "Islamization vs. Politicisation Poses a Dilemma in Pakistan," *Far Eastern Economic Review*, (7 June 1984): 42; and J. Henry Korson and Michelle Maskiell, "Islamization and Social Policy in Pakistan: The Constitutional Crisis and the Status of Women," *Asian Survey* 25, No. 6 (June 1985): 589–612.

11. Personal interview with Mohammad Zia ul-Haq, Rawalpindi, 10 July 1985.

12. Cf. Khalid B. Sayeed, *Politics in Pakistan: The Nature and Direction of Change* (New York: Praeger, 1980); and Louis D. Hayes, *Politics in Pakistan: The Struggle for Legitimacy* (Boulder and London: Westview Press, 1984), 165–83.

13. Cf. William L. Richter, "Pakistan in 1984: Digging In," *Asian Survey* 25, No. 2 (February 1985): 145–54.

Index

ISLAMIC REASSERTION IN PAKISTAN

was composed in 10-point Mergenthaler Linotron 202 Janson and leaded 2 points
by Coghill Book Typesetting Co.;
with display type in Della Robbia by Rochester Mono/Headliners;
and ornaments provided by Job Litho Services;
printed sheet-fed offset on 50-pound, acid-free Warren's Olde Style,
Smyth-sewn and bound over 80-point binder's boards in Holliston Roxite B
by Thomson-Shore, Inc.;
with dust jackets printed in two colors by Philips Offset Company, Inc.;
and published by

SYRACUSE UNIVERSITY PRESS
SYRACUSE, NEW YORK 13244-5160